CULTURES OF THE WORLD

Romania

Cavendish
Square
New York

Published in 2016 by Cavendish Square Publishing, LLC
243 5th Avenue, Suite 136, New York, NY 10016

Library of Congress Cataloging-in-Publication Data

Sheehan, Sean, 1951-
Romania / Sean Sheehan and Debbie Nevins.
pages cm. — (Cultures of the world)
Includes bibliographical references and index.
ISBN 978-1-50260-336-4 (hardcover) ISBN 978-1-50260-337-1 (ebook)
1. Romania—Juvenile literature. I. Nevins, Debbie. II. Title.

DR205.S482 2016
949.8—dc23

2015002700

Writers, Sean Sheehan; Debbie Nevins, third edition
Editorial Director, third edition: David McNamara
Editor, third edition: Debbie Nevins
Art Director, third edition: Jeffrey Talbot
Designer, third edition: Jessica Nevins
Production Manager, third edition: Jennifer Ryder-Talbot
Cover Picture Researcher: Stephanie Flecha
Picture Researcher, third edition: Jessica Nevins

PRECEDING PAGE
A Romanian girl in traditional dress.

Printed in the United States of America

CONTENTS

ROMANIA TODAY

ROMANIA TODAY IS AT AN EXCITING TIME IN ITS HISTORY. IN December 2014, Romania marked the twenty-fifth anniversary of the fall of communism—and twenty-five years of democracy. Those years have been well spent. In just a single generation, the country has undergone a remarkable transformation from dictatorship to freedom. It has instituted free and fair elections, improved living standards, and signaled its new identity as a full-fledged member of Europe. It shed its previous skin as a Soviet bloc satellite country and became a Western-leaning independent nation. In the first decade of the twenty-first century, Romania joined both the European Union (EU) and the North Atlantic Treaty Organization (NATO), which is no small feat given that membership in those organizations is granted only upon clearing a fairly high bar of requirements and standards. In Romania today, the future is bright.

Nevertheless, Romania has a lot of work to do. It is one of the poorest nations in the EU, and like all of Eastern Europe, economically far behind Western Europe. In 2014, the country ranked sixtieth out of 142 on the Legatum Prosperity Index, an annual ranking of the wealth and well-being of most of the world's nations.

In 2012, protesters in Bucharest demonstrate against economic austerity measures that were imposed to help Romania meet its international debt obligations.

(For comparison, that year, Norway ranked number one and the Central African Republic ranked last. Some countries were not included due to the lack of reliable data or other reasons.) This index evaluates a country's performance in the areas of economy, opportunity, governance, education, health, safety, personal freedom, and social capital, and arrives at an overall picture of a society's satisfaction. Romania's numbers put it in the global mid-range, far from the worst, but with plenty of room for improvement. Among the statistics, certain findings tend to stand out. In Romania's case, one of the most concerning topics relates to corruption. According to this index, 79.6 percent of Romanians believe business and or government corruption is widespread.

Indeed, corruption seems to be endemic in the Romanian society, and is proving to be a tough nut to crack. The US Embassy in Bucharest web page states flatly that "Corruption is a serious problem in Romania." Bribery is pervasive. According to Romanian law, receiving a bribe, giving a bribe, accepting undue benefits, and influence trafficking are specifically prohibited. But these laws are not regularly enforced.

Even health care is subject to bribery. Patients often find it necessary to bribe a doctor to attend to their concerns. The practice is so widespread that reportedly standard bribe amounts exist, determined according to the procedure needed. For example, difficult surgeries require higher bribes, often in the thousands of dollars. One reason for this situation is that doctors are paid so little in Romania that they need to take bribes to make a livable income.

Romania's president Klaus Iohannis said during his election campaign that he was determined to tackle the problem of corruption. It won't be easy. Romania's parliament has repeatedly tried to limit anticorruption efforts. Legislators justify such efforts by saying they are being targeted for political reasons and need protection. Whatever the reason, in 2014, sixteen legislators, including seven senators and nine members of the lower house of Parliament, were indicted on corruption charges, along with an army general, four prosecutors, and eighteen judges.

In 2015, Klaus Iohannis became Romania's new president.

Fraud is another concern, as economic crime grows along with the economy. Romania has earned the unwanted reputation as a center for cybercrime, including Internet fraud, credit card fraud, auction site fraud, and hacking and extortion schemes. Young people with savvy Internet skills can, if they are so inclined, make big money in this relatively poor nation.

Such a reputation obviously doesn't help Romania as it works hard to step up in the world. As it is, the country is shaking off an unsavory past, with negative associations to its public image. Even the country's national hero, Vlad III, prince of Walachia, who defended the country against foreign marauders in the fifteenth century, is best known outside Romania as Vlad the Impaler, a medieval sadist famous for his shocking cruelty.

Much more recently, many people still remember the shocking revelations that emerged after the fall of dictator Nicolae Ceausescu in 1989, particularly the scandalous and horrifying conditions in Romanian orphanages. The abuses of that era were not carried out by Ceausescu alone, though, and the deaths and mistreatment of many political prisoners—as well as more than a thousand victims of the secret police during the days of the revolution— weigh heavily on many who are still alive. However, for the most part, they have not been held accountable for their actions. Reaching further back in

Greenpeace activists protest proposed fracking along the Black Sea coast by the US company Chevron.

history, Romania's role in World War II, when it allied itself with the Axis powers, also leaves an ugly scar. Some 250,000 people, mostly Jews and Roma, were deported and killed in keeping with Adolf Hitler's plan.

Today, some say Romanians have a sort of national amnesia about their brutal past. The pain of facing it has made it much easier just to look the other way—to the future. To be sure, the future looks promising. But the ghosts of the past still linger in the shadows of today's Romania, and some people there think the country cannot move forward and truly overcome its problems—corruption being the big one—without facing its distressing past.

The Romanian people today are debating what it is to be Romanian. How should they represent their culture to the world? They want the country they love to stand for something positive, something beautiful, and there is much to work with—charming folk arts, unspoiled landscapes, the gorgeous vistas of the Carpathian Mountains, the quaint towns of Maramures, and the rich diversity of wildlife in the Danube Delta, just to name a few.

Some debates get quite heated, such as those involving the collision of economic versus environmental matters. Should the ancient gold mine in Rosia Montana be opened to a Canadian company to create Europe's largest open-pit gold mine and provide jobs? Or should the project's plans to raze three villages, destroy four mountain tops, and introduce 13,230 tons (12,000 metric tons) of cyanide into the ground each year be reason to stop it? In 2013, thousands of Romanians protested the mining project in fifty cities across the country.

Similarly, Romanians are debating and protesting a plan by foreign companies to extract shale gas by means of fracking, a highly controversial process that contaminates ground water. Chevron and other energy companies have already purchased the extraction rights, including more than two million acres on the Black Sea coast. So far, local protests have held off the drilling.

On a much lighter note, Romanians also grapple with what to do about their country's best-known citizen, the fictitious Count Dracula of Transylvania. Internationally, the character is probably the most recognizable symbol of Romania, and it certainly generates tourism income. But many Romanians feel they've gotten a rotten deal. After all, Dracula is the invention of an Irishman who had never stepped foot in their country, and a character that Hollywood continues to exploit.

A Romanian shopkeeper holds up a Dracula figure, one of many items for sale at her souvenir shop.

In 2001, Romania's minister of tourism proposed the construction of a Dracula theme park in the medieval town of Sighisoara in Transylvania. Aside from being a perfect backdrop for the Dracula story, the town is also the birthplace of a different, and real, Dracula, the bloodthirsty, fifteenth-century Vlad Dracula, aka Vlad the Impaler. Many Romanians were ready to jump in on the project, figuring out ways that they could profit off the Dracula brand. But many others were less enthusiastic, and the project was ultimately voted down.

Must Romania be forever associated with the blood-sipping, black-caped count? Time will tell. Meanwhile, Romania's tourism sector offers plenty of uplifting alternatives, from wine and food tours to folk festivals to bird watching in the Danube Delta. The new Romania—whatever form it takes— is in the hands of the Romanian people to create, nurture, and promote.

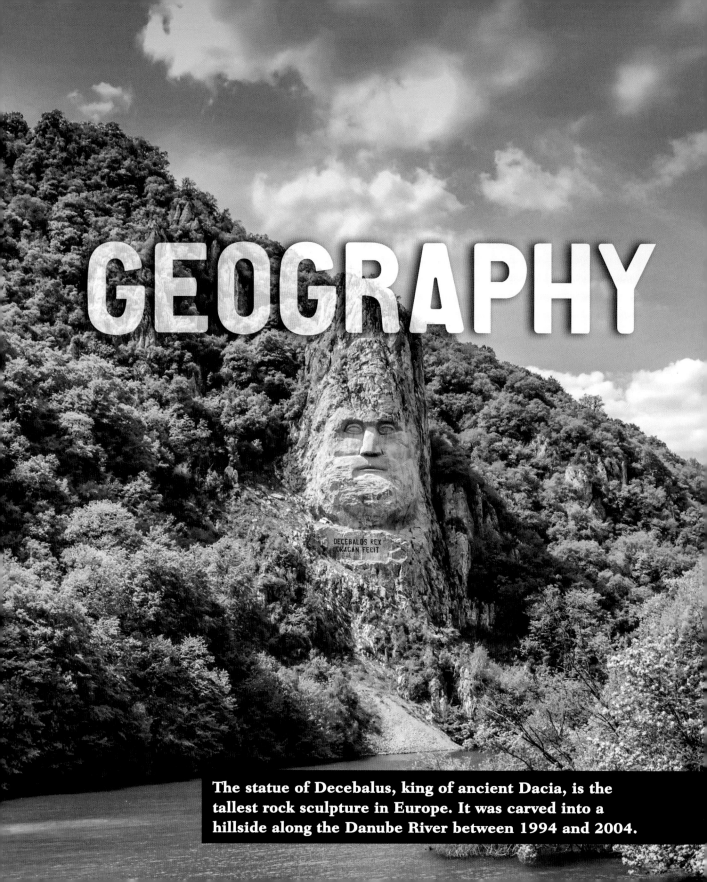

GEOGRAPHY

The statue of Decebalus, king of ancient Dacia, is the tallest rock sculpture in Europe. It was carved into a hillside along the Danube River between 1994 and 2004.

ROMANIA IS SHAPED SOMETHING like a giant fist in southeastern Europe, with its thumb tucked in at the top and its wrist extending into the Black Sea. It's the twelfth-largest country in Europe and, situated on the northern part of the Balkan Peninsula, the largest in the Balkan region. It covers 91,700 square miles (237,500 square kilometers), and is a little smaller than the state of Oregon. It is bordered (starting in the north and going clockwise) by Ukraine, Moldova, the Black Sea, Bulgaria, Serbia, and Hungary.

About one-third of the country is covered by the Carpathian Mountains, which surround the large Transylvanian Basin, a plateau in the west of the country. Beyond the mountain ranges to the south and east, the mighty Danube River and its tributaries enrich extensive plains that make up another third of the country.

CARPATHIAN MOUNTAINS

The Carpathian Mountains stretch some 700 miles (1,800 km) across Romanian territory, forming a curve around Transylvania, a historical region in the central part of the country, and then separating into three

1

At 59 miles (96 km) long, the Danube–Black Sea Canal in southeastern Romania is the world's third-longest man-made navigation route after the Suez and the Panama canals.

Capra Lake is one of the glacial lakes in the Transylvanian Alps.

main ranges. The highest range, the Southern Carpathians, is commonly known as the Transylvanian Alps because of the many glacial features found there. A typical feature is a cirque, a steep-sided hollow caused by glacial erosion, which is usually found at the head of a mountain valley. Many cirques have been carved into the sides of the Transylvanian Alps. There are also more than 150 beautiful glacial lakes, a testimony to the last Ice Age. The highest point in the country, Mount Moldoveanu at 8,346 feet (2,544 m), is found in these Alps.

The Eastern Carpathians include zones of sandstone ridges, limestone formations, and volcanic ranges. Imposing river gorges wind their way through these mountains, flanked by limestone walls that reach heights of more than 300 feet (91.4 m). The volcanic zone, composed mainly of long-dead craters and cones, is heavily forested with commercial plantations of conifer trees.

The Western Carpathians are the lowest in elevation and contain many of the largest caves in the country. Evidence of human habitation going back

Most of the Carpathian Mountains are composed of hard crystalline and volcanic rocks. But some mountainous regions are made of limestone and granite, which make them more susceptible to erosion. Bizarrely shaped rock formations, mighty gorges, and spectacular river valleys have developed, giving the mountains a fascinating appeal for both geologists and tourists.

Over thousands of years, erosion carved out a number of caves in the Southern Carpathians. Water percolating through limestone formed underground channels and rivers that eventually flow to the surface, creating a landscape known as karst. *Erosion under the surface continues, and intricate cave systems develop as a result.*

A Romanian biologist and zoologist, Emil Racovita (1868–1947), contributed a great deal to the study of caves, a science called speleology. He explored more than 1,400 caves throughout Europe, studying life forms in underground environments. He also established the world's first speleological institute at what is today named Babeş-Bolyai University, Romania's largest such institution.

to the Stone Age has been found in mountain caves in Romania. Unlike the other two Carpathian ranges, the Western Carpathians are not a continuous range. They are characterized by clusters of mountains in a north—south direction, separated by deep gorges. These gorges have served as strategically important sites, or gates, for gaining access to or defending the region. This function is reflected in their names, like the famous Iron Gates on the Danube.

The mountains provide some of the most attractive scenery Romania has to offer. This, plus the wealth of wildlife, helps explain why the first national parks in Romania were established in the Southern Carpathians in the 1930s. One

Beautiful scenery is everywhere in Retezat National Park.

of the biggest, the Retezat National Park, covers an area of more than 94,016 acres (38,047 hectares) and includes more than eighty lakes of glacial origin.

FLORA AND FAUNA

Romania has a wide variety of plant and animal life. In the Retezat National Park in the Southern Carpathians, for example, more than 1,200 species of plants have been recorded. Mountainous areas, densely covered with woods, are inhabited by animals like the brown bear and wild boar, which are becoming increasingly rare in other parts of Europe. Quite common in the Southern Carpathians, above the tree line, is a mountain goat known as the chamois. Its skin makes a soft leather also called chamois.

Some of the most exciting wildlife lives in the Danube Delta region, where millions of birds spend the winter or stop over during their annual migrations. The delta is equidistant from the equator and the North Pole, and makes a

natural resting and feeding point for birds before they fly on to northern Europe, China, Siberia, and parts of Africa. Consequently, the Danube Delta is rich in bird and animal species, and some three hundred kinds of birds arrive on a regular basis. Visitors include the Egyptian vulture, the black-winged stilt roller, and the pygmy cormorant.

A cow watches a pelican take flight in the biologically rich environment of the Danube Delta.

The upper reaches of the delta, where the water doesn't cover everything, provides a home to a variety of mammals, such as mink, muskrats, foxes, and wild cats. Various snakes—many of them poisonous—live in colonies on some of the larger islands. In addition, there are about thirty species of bats found across the land, twenty-two of which live within the country's eighty-five caves.

The Danube Delta covers 1,950 square miles (5,050 sq km), of which 1,750 square miles (4,532 sq km) are in Romania. It has been designated a United Nations Educational, Scientific, and Cultural Organization (UNESCO) World Heritage Site.

The Dobrogea has a dry plateau ringed by mountains.

FLATLANDS

Flatlands, or plateaus, are elevated areas of land that are often flat on the surface and bounded by steep sides. Most of Transylvania is a large plateau enclosed by the arc of the Carpathian Mountains. Large deposits of methane gas provide the region with its most valuable resource and make the plateau one of Romania's most prosperous regions. Many salt lakes and hot springs are found in the Transylvanian Basin, giving rise to numerous spas and health resorts.

Beyond the mountains are more flatlands. To the east of the Eastern Carpathians, in the northeast of Romania, is the Moldavian Plateau. This is an important area for grain and sugar beet production, and the steep hills are mined for their granite and quartz.

The part of Romania that lies between the Danube and the Black Sea, called Dobrogea (DOH-bro-jah), also has a plateau formed from eroded rock. The average altitude here is 820 feet (250 m), and while there is little potential for agriculture because of the hot and dry climate, granite quarrying is a major activity.

THE MIGHTY DANUBE

The Danube River is one of the world's greatest rivers. It is the second longest in Europe, and carries an average of fifty million tons (45 million t) of alluvial deposits every year. It begins in Germany's Black Forest and flows through Austria, Hungary, Serbia, and Ukraine; forms parts of the southern border with both Serbia and Bulgaria; then enters Romania and meanders sluggishly to the Black Sea. The Danube's 668-mile (1,075 km) course through Romania to the Black Sea is completely navigable. For countless centuries, the river was a natural barrier in the south of Romania because of its tremendous width of over 2 miles (3.2 km). Between the years 103 and 105 CE, under orders from the Emperor Trajan, the Romans constructed a bridge across the Danube at the town of Drobeta-Turnu Severin, which is located in southern Romania.

A few miles upstream lies the huge Iron Gate I Hydroelectric Power Station dam that harnesses the Danube's power as it flows through the rapids that separate Romania and Serbia. Since the completion of the dam and its lock gates in 1971, the rapids of the Iron Gate no longer present a formidable hazard to navigators. But upstream, the Kazan Gorge remains a spectacular and daunting phenomenon. There the river flows fast, twisting and turning as it gushes through a narrow gorge with cliffs more than 2,000 feet (610 m) high.

In 1999, river transport became difficult following the bombing of three bridges in Serbia during the Kosovo War. The resulting debris was finally cleared in 2002 and a temporary pontoon bridge, which further hampered river traffic, was removed in 2005.

Most of Romania's other rivers are tributaries of the Danube. All tributaries—the Olt, Jiu, Arges, and Ialomita—flow across the plains of Walachia. The second longest river, the Mures, flows westward into Hungary, where it joins another tributary of the great Danube.

The Iron Gate I Hydroelectric Power Station dam

THE PLAINS

Plains are areas of flat or gently rolling ground often formed by deposits from rivers, glaciers, or the sea. They form about one-third of Romania's landmass and characterize much of the land in the south, in the region known as Walachia (Va-LAH-hiah). The Olt River, which runs from the north to the south through the southern part of the country, divides the Walachian Plain in two. West of the Olt River is

The plains of Romania have rich soil for farming.

the Oltenian Plain, which reaches a maximum elevation of 984 feet (300 m), while east of the river lies the Romanian Plain. The plains are covered by loess, wind-blown deposits of silt that make very fertile farmland if there is adequate rainfall or irrigation. Romanian farmers depend on dams for irrigation. Farther south, nearer the Danube River, former marshland has been drained, and the rich alluvial soil is suited for crops such as rice and tomatoes. The Walachian Plains are made up of vast fields, where farmers grow most of the country's wheat and corn.

THE DANUBE DELTA

The triangular Danube Delta, where the river runs into the Black Sea in the southeast of the country, is formed by three tributaries of the Danube River. The area that now makes up the delta was once a bay that over thousands of years became filled with mud and sediment carried by the waters of the Danube.

The delta's economic importance is derived from its rich potential for fishing. Half the country's fish come from the delta, which is rich in carp and supplies 90 percent of the sturgeon catch. The eggs of the female sturgeon are used to make caviar, an expensive food considered to have a superior taste to other roe.

The delta has many floating reed islands, formed by large and small collections of reeds rooted together by their rhizomes. The reeds serve an economic purpose. They are harvested, pulped, and then the cellulose content is used for making paper and textiles.

Because the delta-building process is ongoing, the land annually moves several yards into the Black Sea. Approximately 13 to 16 percent of the delta is made up of dry land that is covered by softwood forests, shrubs, and woody vines, which help to give the delta a tropical appearance.

CLIMATE

Romania's climate is a temperate continental one, with hot summers and cold winters. The average temperature in July is 70 degrees Fahrenheit (21 degrees Celsius), while in January it drops to slightly below freezing. Icy winds sweep down from Russia in winter, and widespread snowfall is common. Variations in altitude, however, account for regional differences. The plains are usually warmer than the mountainous areas, and precipitation—rain and snowfall— can reach 40 inches (101 centimeters) in the mountains, twice that of the plains. Generally speaking, the climate is well suited for agriculture.

The effects of severe flooding in the Romanian town of Tecuci in September 2007 can be seen in this aerial view.

A view of a bustling Bucharest is reflected in the Dambovita River.

CITIES

The cities of Romania are a mixture of ancient and modern.

BUCHAREST The capital of Romania, Bucharest (Boo-koo-RESHT), lies on the banks of the Dambovita River, in the southeast of the country in the Walachia region. First mentioned in a fifteenth-century document, it is now home to nearly 1.95 million inhabitants. In its heyday between World War I and World War II, the elegant capital was known as the "Paris of the East" or "Little Paris," but since then it has lost some of its glory. During the regime of dictator Nicolae Ceausescu (in office 1965—1989), many historic areas of the city were demolished and replaced by huge utilitarian structures in a program called systematization. Since that era, Bucharest has worked to restore and bring life back to historic parts of the city.

BRASOV Brasov (BRAH-shov) was founded by the medieval Saxons in Transylvania and still retains the old streets and buildings that evoke its Gothic past. However, in the years after 1945, thousands of villagers from

Moldova settled in Brasov. Factories and blocks of apartments were built and the city is now an industrial center with around 277,000 people. Textiles, food products, light industries producing farm machinery and electrical equipment, and the oil and chemical industries provide employment for many of the inhabitants. Brasov is also a winter sports center and resort.

Red roofs shine in Brasov's historic city center.

CONSTANTA Constanta (Kohn-STAHN-tsah) on the Black Sea coast is almost as large as Brasov. It has important commercial and transportation links to the capital, which lies about 165 miles (265 km) to the east. Constanta is Romania's major seaport—well over 50 percent of the country's exports pass through its port facilities—and it is the second biggest commercial center on the Black Sea. The city is also developing into an industrial center with packaging, food processing, shipbuilding, and metallurgical industries.

INTERNET LINKS

romaniatourism.com/geography.html
Romania's tourism site has an overview of the country's geography.

travel.nationalgeographic.com/travel/countries/romania-guide
See the Romania photo galleries on this National Geographic site.

www.spurfilm.eu/transylvania-romania/transylvania.html
A Transylvanian film company offers a nice section on the geography and history of Transylvania.

retezat.ro
The site of the Retezat National Park has beautiful photo galleries. Choose English language for navigating.

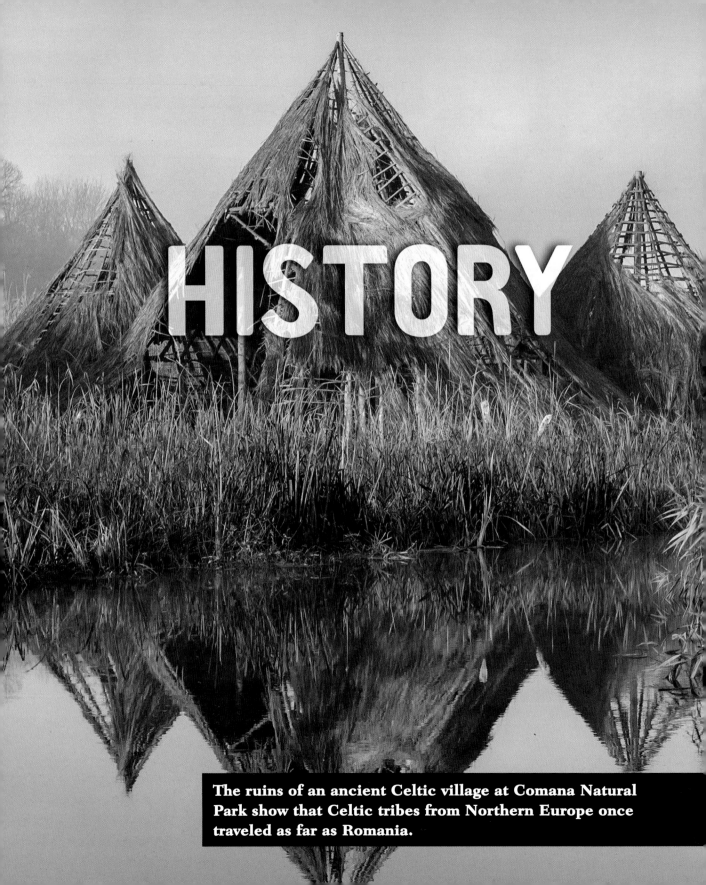

HISTORY

The ruins of an ancient Celtic village at Comana Natural Park show that Celtic tribes from Northern Europe once traveled as far as Romania.

2

ROMANIA HAS SEEN HARD TIMES. For nearly two thousand years, this part of Eastern Europe has been subject to conquest and rule by foreign empires. In fact, Romania itself didn't come into being until 1877, when the united principalities of Walachia and Moldavia were formally recognized as an independent state. Even after independence, the history of present-day Romania—consisting of Walachia, Moldavia, and Transylvania—was clouded by fear and oppression. In 1989, when its own dictatorship was overthrown, the country began a radical new era.

THE ROMANS ARRIVE

When the Romans moved into what is now Romania in 101 CE, they were conquering a region called Dacia. The Greeks had established colonies along the Black Sea, but since they never moved inland, Greek culture made little impact on the local population.

The Dacians became subjects of the Roman Empire in 106 CE. Barely two hundred years later, between 271 to 275 CE, Emperor

Vlad III, Prince of Walachia in the fifteenth century, is hailed as a Romanian hero. But he is also called Vlad the Impaler, who was shockingly sadistic to his enemies. He is said to be the model for the fictional Transylvanian vampire Count Dracula in Bram Stoker's 1897 horror novel, *Dracula*.

Aurelian ordered the withdrawal of troops and administrators from the province because of the increasing cost of defending the region from barbarian tribes—a variety of Goths, Huns, Slavs, Mongols, and others. Despite their short time in Dacia, the Romans had a significant impact. Some Roman settlers remained and intermarried with the Dacians, who adopted Roman customs and the Latin language. Early forms of Christianity were introduced when Christianity became the official religion of the Roman Empire in the fourth century.

The Densus medieval church in Tara Hategului is the oldest church in Romania where services are still held.

THE THREE PRINCIPALITIES

From the third to the eleventh centuries, the Dacian region faced invasions of migratory peoples, including the Magyars (ethnic Hungarians) and Slavs. The people in the region relied on the local *voivode* (VO-e-vod), or military leader, to protect them. In exchange, they gave their allegiance to him, paid tribute, and provided soldiers in times of danger. In 1330 several small voivodates in the south united under the leadership of Prince Basarab to establish the principality of Walachia. In 1359 the nobility in the east came together under the leadership of Prince Bogdan I. They built their settlements near the Moldova River.

Over time and a process of assimilation, the Romanian people emerged. From the Middle Ages to the present, the Romanians lived in three adjoining principalities: Walachia, Moldavia, and Transylvania. From the eleventh to the twentieth centuries, Transylvania was part of the Hungarian Kingdom. During this period, Walachia and Moldavia became religiously and culturally aligned to the Eastern Orthodox practices of the Byzantine Empire.

TRANSYLVANIA

Transylvania has switched hands numerous times in its history, dominated by different peoples and countries over the centuries. Sometimes it has been part of Romania, and sometimes not. There are two histories of Transylvania, the Romanian and the Hungarian versions, each of which claims the territory was first settled by their people.

Whoever came first, they were joined by Germanic settlers known as Saxons, who also stayed in the region. The ruling nobility was mainly made up of Europeans, including Magyars, or ethnic Hungarians. They received the support of the Austrian Habsburg Empire, which involved the kingdom of Hungary. Despite a revolt

by Romanian peasants in 1784 and 1785, Hungarian influence was reinforced in the years that followed. During the nineteenth century, the kingdom of Hungary began a policy of Magyarization, the implementation of Hungarian culture in the region, with the intention of making it the dominant culture. Hungarian became the official language.

When Romania entered World War I in 1916, on the side of the Allies fighting against the Austro-Hungarian Empire, it attacked Hungarian forces in Transylvania. After the war, the empire collapsed, and Romania reclaimed Transylvania. Adolf Hitler then gave part of Transylvania back to Hungary in the Second Vienna Award of 1940 during World War II (1939–1945). Finally, the Allies won the war and Transylvania was once again fully reunited with Romania in 1947, where it remains today.

After centuries of shifting rule, with its conflicting loyalties, opposition, and repression, relations between the Transylvanian ethnic Romanian majority and the Hungarian minority remain strained. Both Romania and Hungary still claim Transylvania as their own territory.

They also based their written laws on the Byzantine codes. Occasional conflicts affected the stability of the principalities. In 1437 the Romanian population in Transylvania was reduced to the status of serfs after a peasant rebellion against the Magyar and Saxon nobles. The kingdoms of Hungary and Poland had designs on the principalities of Walachia and Moldavia, causing unrest among the nobility. The greatest threat of all, and the one that would prove most significant, came from the south, where the mighty Ottoman Empire was making its ascendance.

OVERCOME BY THE TURKS

The fourteenth and fifteenth centuries were marked by the Romanians' struggle to withstand the onslaught of Ottoman rule. The Ottoman kingdom was an Islamic state founded by Turkish tribes in 1299. Over the next three centuries, the Turks conquered southeast Europe, much of the Middle East, western Asia, and coastal North Africa, culminating in a vast empire that reached its zenith in the sixteenth century.

Though Romania tried to hold it off, the Ottoman power prevailed. Romanians identify many of their heroes from this period. Before Walachia succumbed, Alexander the Good of Moldavia (r. 1401—1431) led a defiant resistance, as did Vlad III, the Prince of Walachia (r. 1448, 1456—1462, 1476) and Stephen the Great (r. 1457—1504). Stephen the Great defeated the Hungarians and Poles as well as the Turks. He is also famous for building monasteries and churches in Moldavia, eight of which are today listed as a UNESCO World Heritage Site.

It was during Ottoman rule that the three principalities of Walachia, Moldavia, and Transylvania were first united under Michael the Brave of Walachia. Michael's conquest of Transylvania in 1600 proved brief, and resistance to Turkish rule soon crumbled after he was assassinated in 1601. Other princes, who had no qualms about accepting the yoke of foreign domination, went down in Romanian history labeled with epithets such as Basil the Locust, Ion the Cruel, and Aron the Tyrant.

VLAD DRACULA, SON OF THE DRAGON

One of the most fascinating figures in Romanian history is Vlad III, Prince of Walachia (1431–1476). Romanians celebrate him as a folk hero who valiantly fought the Ottoman aggressors. He was a member of the House of Draculesti, and was known as Vlad Draculea, *or Vlad Dracula. His father, Vlad II Dracul, was a member of the Order of the Dragon, a fellowship of knights dedicated to protecting Christianity in Eastern Europe. (*Dracul *means "dragon," or sometimes, "devil.")*

When he was eleven, Vlad and his younger brother Radu were taken captive by the Ottoman Sultan Murad II. The boys were held as hostages to ensure cooperation from their father, who was the voivode, or military governor, of Walachia. Meanwhile, the Turks educated the boys in Ottoman culture as well as in the arts of war. Radu embraced his new culture, converted to Islam, and would go on to fight for the sultan—and against his brother. Vlad, however, hated his captors, and once he was freed, he reclaimed his father's position as ruler of Walachia and fought against the Ottomans.

Vlad III is hailed as a fair-minded and courageous man who fought for his land's independence from both the Ottomans and the Hungarians. However, he was also astonishingly brutal to his enemies. Literature from the era accuses him of employing a number of horrifying punishments, especially that of impaling his captives on long spikes. Although not all of the dreadful stories can be verified, it seems that he did indeed earn his gruesome nickname, Vlad the Impaler.

A NATION EMERGES

King Carol I

During the late 1700s, the Turks suffered military defeats by the Russian and Habsburg armies, and Turkey began to lose its influence. (The Habsburg dynasty, based in Austria, was one of the most important and powerful royal houses, or extended royal families, in Europe.) As Ottoman power declined, Russia and the Habsburg monarchy squabbled for parts of the region. In 1821 there was a popular rebellion in Walachia against the Phanariot Greek rulers who had been governing the region under the auspices of the Ottoman Empire. The leader of the uprising, Tudor Vladimirescu, stirred nationalist emotions to a new pitch before he was executed.

Meanwhile, skirmishes and wars were going on throughout the region, and the Romanian principalities were caught in the middle of them. The Greeks waged a war of independence against Ottoman rule in 1821, and Russia supported the Greeks because it wanted to get the Turks out of the Black Sea area; Russia wanted that region for itself. The wars ended with the Treaty of Adrianople in 1829, which granted Russian rule over the Romanian principalities. The new regime granted some autonomy to Romanian nobles in return for them supporting Russia and not the Austrian Empire of the Habsburg monarchy. By 1834 the region was sufficiently stable for Russian troops to withdraw.

The idea of uniting Walachia and Moldavia had been developing throughout the period of Turkish rule, and the time was now ripe for its realization. In 1859 Prince Alexandru Ioan Cuza was elected as head of Walachia and Moldavia. In 1866 these principalities became collectively known as Romania, or *Rumania* as it was then spelled. A new ruler, Prince Carol, emerged in 1866. Eleven years into his rule, he led a combined Romanian and Russian army that defeated the Turks at the Battle of Plevna. At the Congress of Berlin in 1878, Turkish rule officially came to an end. Soon after, in 1881, Prince Carol became King Carol I, the first king of Romania. (Carol is Romanian for "Charles.")

WORLD WAR I AND ITS AFTERMATH

After centuries of foreign rule, Romanians finally had their own constitution. However, for the peasants who made up the majority of the population, life remained harsh. A feudal system still existed in Romania, and the large landowners, despite their small numbers, wielded much political power. The peasants' plight was ignored by the nobility-led Romanian government, which was more anxious to make deals with Western European capitalists interested in exploiting Romania's natural resources. In 1907 a rural uprising occurred, and rich estates were attacked and burned. The army crushed the rebellion, killing ten thousand peasants, and an uneasy peace was restored.

In 1914, when World War I erupted, Ferdinand I succeeded Carol I. At the end of the war in 1920, the victorious Allies dismantled the empires of losing side: Germany, Austria-Hungary, and the Ottoman Empire, and redrew the map of Europe. The Allies wanted to strengthen Romania at the expense of neighboring Hungary, because of the Austria-Hungarian empire's aggressive role in WWI. The Trianon Treaty doubled the size of Romania, uniting it with

King Ferdinand inspects his troops during WWI.

Six-year-old King Michael and his three regents take the oath of loyalty in 1927.

Transylvania, Bucovina (now in southern Ukraine), and Bessarabia (now the Republic of Moldova). By 1920, Romania was more than twice the size it had been in 1914. Naturally, Hungary was displeased with this new arrangement. Transylvania, made up of a majority of 2,800,000 Romanians, also contained a significant minority of 1,600,000 Hungarian Magyars. At the time, however, Hungary had no choice but to accept the plan.

In the years following World War I, Greater Romania was a liberal constitutional monarchy, with about 28 percent of the population made up of various minority groups: Magyars, Jews, Germans, Ukrainians, Bulgarians, and others. Romania's constitution, enacted in 1923 and called the "Constitution of Union," guaranteed equal rights for all, freedom of expression and assembly, of conscience, and of religion, although it did declare Romanian Orthodox Catholicism to be the dominant religion.

Yet those years were far from peaceful for Romania. Social unrest developed, made worse by imperialist threats from the newly-formed Soviet Union, a Russia-dominated union of Communist states which bordered Romania. In addition, the rise of authoritarian, ultra-conservative, nationalistic groups called fascists added political and social pressures, as did the economic collapse of the Great Depression of 1929—1933. Massive unemployment encouraged support for the fascists, who blamed non-ethnic Romanians and the communists for the country's problems.

King Ferdinand's son, Crown Prince Carol, was next in line to become king of Romania. However, Carol's various marriages, divorces, and affairs scandalized the country, so he renounced his right to the throne. Instead, his six-year-old son Michael became king in 1927. In royal tradition, when the monarch is too young to rule, a regent or groups of regents act as a substitute, governing in his name until he comes of age. But after three years of regency rule, the Romanian prime minister engineered a coup d'état (koo day-tah), or overthrow of the government. Carol returned and took the throne.

Carol II became king in 1930 and reigned for ten years, but he failed to tackle the country's social and economic problems. As a new war loomed in Europe, and fascist, antisemitic groups gained strength—particularly the Iron Guard party in Romania—Carol might have felt that he was losing control of his country. For example, after his prime minister Ion Duca banned the Iron Guard in 1933 and attempted to repress the group through police arrests, beatings, torture, and killings, Iron Guard members promptly assassinated Duca.

In 1938, the king abolished the Parliament and put a harsh new constitution in force, severely limiting rights and freedoms, and giving himself supreme power. In his role as a dictator, Carol II banned political parties, "revolutionary propaganda," and, working through his new Prime Minister Armand Calinescu, secretly arranged in 1939 for the execution of the leader of the Iron Guard. History was chillingly repeated when the Iron Guard then assassinated Calinescu.

When the constitution was put in place in 1938, it was pasted on the walls throughout Romania, like this one in Bucharest, for all to read.

WORLD WAR II

When World War II broke out in 1939, Romania was a deeply divided country. At first, Carol attempted to maintain Romanian neutrality in the war but was unable to enforce it. In 1940, as the Axis forces of Nazi Germany and Fascist Italy extended their power across Europe, they negotiated the Second Vienna Award. This agreement transferred a large part of Translyvania and other Romanian territories back to Hungary. Meanwhile, the Soviet Union annexed Romania's Bessarabia and Bucovina territories. Bowing to Romanian outrage, Carol was forced to abdicate and his son Michael once again became king.

But the real power was in the hands of General Ion Antonescu. The antisemitic Antonescu supported Germany, which was purging Europe of Jews and other "unwanted" populations. Romania joined Germany in the invasion of Russia in 1941—whereas in World War I, Romania had been allied with Russia against Germany,

General Ion Antonescu met with his ally, German leader Adolf Hitler, in Munich in June 1941.

now the tables had turned and Romania became allied with the Axis.

Under Antonescu, pogroms, or massacres, were organized within Romania. Some 300,000 Jews were executed or deported. King Michael deposed Antonescu in August 1944, just as Russian troops crossed the border and occupied Romania. (In 1946, after the war, the Romanian government found Antonescu guilty of war crimes and executed him.)

Consequently, there was a powerful Soviet influence in the government of Romania after the end of the war in 1945. Most of Romania's confiscated land was returned after World War II, and there was a significant change in land reform policy that affected millions of peasants. Women were given the right to vote in 1946, and the monarchy was abolished. Soviet authorities forced King Michael to abdicate, or step down, in 1947; Romania was declared a People's Republic, and Petru Groza headed the puppet communist government. (A puppet government does the bidding of a stronger foreign government.)

THE YEARS OF COMMUNISM

Romania became a satellite state of the Soviet Union. The government, the economy, and the educational system were drastically reworked to resemble the Soviet system. Stalinist principles—imposed by Joseph Stalin, the brutal leader of the Soviet Union—were introduced in Romania and remained in place until the late 1980s.

All industries, commercial enterprises, and banks were nationalized and placed under the control of the government. In the countryside, farmland was collectivized against the wishes of the majority of peasants, resulting in protests and the arrest of thousands. Collectivization meant that farmers no longer owned the land they worked, and small farms were forced to combine into large collectives under the control and management of the government.

In 1965, Nicolae Ceausescu (nee-kaw-LY-a Chow-SHESS-koo) became the leader of the Romanian Communist Party, and then of the country. His government became one of the most repressive, rigid, and brutal of all the harsh communist regimes under Soviet control.

Nicolae Ceausescu addresses his congress in November 1989.

Dissent against the communist regime was not allowed. Churches, especially those belonging to ethnic minorities that refused to cooperate with government policies, were disbanded. Political prisoners spent their time in jail or were sent to work on labor projects, such as the Danube—Black Sea Canal, where the work was so dangerous it became known as the Canal of Death. The project claimed the lives of more than 100,000 workers.

Romania did occasionally express its sense of independence by opposing the policies of the Soviet Union. Romania's Communist Party refused to support the Soviet Union's invasion of Czechoslovakia in 1968 and of Afghanistan in 1981. A more symbolic gesture of independence was the country's decision to send a national team to the 1984 Los Angeles Olympics, defying the Soviet Union's boycott of the Games that year.

Nicolae Ceausescu and his wife, Elena, were executed on Christmas Day 1989. The event was marked by a celebratory spirit across the country, a reaction that many outsiders found difficult to understand until details of Ceausescu's regime of terror came to be general knowledge.

Ceausescu came from a poor family, and after a very elementary education he began an apprenticeship as a shoemaker. He became interested in politics and rose quickly through the ranks of the Communist Party to become its general secretary in 1965. He became Romania's president two years later. As leader of the country, Ceausescu made many political maneuvers to ensure that he stayed in power. He appointed members of his family, notably his wife, to fill key leadership positions. He also gave the impression of being in opposition to Soviet authority by meeting with many Western leaders, including US president Richard Nixon, who visited Romania in 1969.

Behind the glamour, however, Ceausescu presided over a dreadful tyranny. Foreign books and movies were banned, and even typewriters had to be registered with the police. Individuals buying paper were likely to be interrogated by the state security police, the Securitate *(SAE-ku-ri-TA-teh). The Securitate also enforced restrictions such as limiting families to only one forty-watt bulb per apartment. In 1981 Romanians were subject to bread rationing, and measures were taken to limit the consumption of basic foodstuffs, such as sugar, coffee, and flour, while food was exported in an effort to pay off Romania's large foreign debt. Ceausescu's heavy-handed debt-reduction policies resulted in massive shortages of food, fuel, and medicines in the country. While most of the population suffered terrible hardship during this time, the Ceausescus lived luxuriously, as tyrants usually do.*

Romanians take to the streets in celebration after the execution of Nicolae Ceausescu.

POPULAR REVOLUTION

In December 1989, thousands of people gathered in the city of Timisoara to protest the worsening of food shortages and to call for a relaxation of the controls exercised by the Ceausescu regime. There had been earlier protests in 1987, but those were stifled by a combination of police repression and a speedy supply of extra food to the neediest regions. This time Ceausescu chose to rely entirely on his security forces and ordered them to fire on demonstrators. Hundreds of protesters died. As news of this spread across the country, other protests spontaneously erupted. In Bucharest, security troops again fired on unarmed crowds. As the death toll went up, the mass protests continued. When some army units refused to carry out government orders, the protests turned into a popular revolution.

As citizens and the army fought with security forces, Ceausescu and his wife fled from the capital but were soon captured by the army. After a hurried trial conducted by a military tribunal, they were found guilty of murder and were executed by a firing squad, all in one day.

Romanians in Timisoara wave flags from which they had cut out the communist coat of arms.

LOOKING TO THE WEST

After the revolution, free elections were held for the first time in 1990. While Romanians voted for change, they did so cautiously. Gradually the country learned how to be a democracy. The 1991 constitution established Romania as a republic with a multiparty system, market economy, and individual rights of free speech, religion, and private ownership.

Since the collapse of the Soviet Union in 1991, Romania has developed closer ties with Western Europe. In 2001, Parliament approved a law aimed at returning properties that had been nationalized during the communist era. In 2004, Romania became a member of the North Atlantic Treaty Organization (NATO). NATO is a political and military alliance of twenty-right member nations (as of 2014), including Canada and the United States. This membership signals a huge change for Romania, as NATO membership ensures security against outside forces, such as the increasingly powerful Russia, which invaded Romania's neighbor Ukraine in 2014. (Ukraine was not a NATO member.)

A giant flag of the European Union is spread across the lawns in front of the parliament building in Bucharest to mark Europe Day on May 9, 2013

Further strengthening its connection to Western Europe, Romania became a part of the European Union in 2007. The EU is an economic and political partnership between twenty-eight European nations (as of 2014). It was created in the aftermath of WWII to foster a sense of interdependence and unity among European nations in order to deter future conflicts. In order to be a part of the EU, a member state must abide by its standards for human rights, freedoms, democracy, and equality.

In 2003, Romania adopted a new constitution to bring its government into line with these standards. Romania hopes its entry into these organizations will bring about greater democracy and economic prosperity, but it hasn't been easy. Romania still struggles with high-level corruption, organized crime, and the still-fresh memories of years of governmental oppression and persecution.

INTERNET LINKS

news.bbc.co.uk/2/hi/europe/country_profiles/1058027.stm
BBC News "Timeline: Romania" covers the period from WWI to the present.

www.rotravel.com/History/Introduction
Romanian Travel Guide has a good section on the country's history.

www.lonelyplanet.com/romania/history
Lonely Planet offers a good overview of Romanian history.

www.newworldencyclopedia.org/entry/transylvania
New World Encyclopedia has an in-depth entry about Transylvania.

GOVERNMENT

The Romanian Senate meets in the Palace of the Parliament in Bucharest in 2014.

3

ROMANIA IS A REPUBLIC WITH A democratically elected bicameral (two-house) parliament and an elected president. The government consists of three main branches: legislative, executive, and judicial.

Under the 1991 constitution, Romania is "a sovereign, independent, unitary, and indivisible National State." All citizens are deemed equal, "without any discrimination on account of race, nationality, ethnic origin, language, religion, sex, opinion, political adherence, property, or social origin." The constitution especially heeds the rights and liberties of individuals because it was drawn up after a legacy of more than

An elderly woman stands in front of a campaign poster for Prime Minister Victor Ponta during the 2014 presidential election. Ponta lost to Klaus Iohannis.

During his 1992 concert tour, pop star Michael Jackson reportedly stood on an outdoor stage at the Romanian Palace of the Parliament in Bucharest and addressed the crowd, saying, "Hello, Budapest!" It was an embarrassing goof—Budapest is the capital of Hungary, not Romania. Since then, other rock stars and celebrities have evidently made the same mistake.

New Romanian president Klaus Iohannis and his wife stand during the inaugural ceremony in December 2014.

forty years of dictatorship. It is similar to the constitution of the United States in that it greatly emphasizes individual freedoms.

As Romania prepared to enter the European Union in 2007, it revised its constitution to bring it in line with EU standards and regulations. It included strengthening Parliament's control over government; restricting parliamentarian immunity; stating more clearly minority rights; recognizing the multiparty political system as a condition of democracy; and guaranteeing the protection of private property from nationalization and other forms of forced transfer.

THE PRESIDENT

The office of president was first introduced in 1974 by Nicolae Ceausescu as a way of consolidating his own power. When the new constitution was being drawn up, there was heated debate over the issue of retaining a president or choosing a form of government known as a constitutional monarchy. The latter was the system that operated in Romania until 1947, and it could have been reintroduced as part of a democratically elected parliamentary system.

In 1990, the Romanian parliament voted to adopt a form of republican government with a president elected by universal suffrage. In 2003 the term of office for the president was changed to five years, with a two-term maximum. The president's powers are clearly defined in the areas of national defense, security, and foreign affairs. The president is the supreme commander of the armed forces, and the chairperson of the Supreme Defense Council. He also plays a major role in representing Romania abroad. The president also promulgates the laws passed by the parliament, and takes action during domestic and international crises. The president is the head of state, but not the head of government; that position is held by the prime minister.

A PALACE FIT FOR A KING—OR A PRESIDENT

In 1883, King Carol I ordered the building of a new palace on Cotroceni Hill in Bucharest. For centuries, it had been the site of a monastery and the residence of previous rulers. The palace was completed in 1895 and served as the residence for Carol and his heirs to the throne. In the twentieth century, further improvements and additions were added.

During the years of communist rule, some of the palace's original ornamentation was destroyed and more than a thousand objects, including paintings, sculptures, furniture, carpets, and other decorative items, went missing or were given away. In 1977, an earthquake struck the Bucharest region and caused great damage to the palace. It has since been renovated.

Since 1991, Cotroceni Palace has served as the residence of the Romanian president. It also houses the National Cotroceni Museum, which is open to the public.

In December 2014, Klaus Iohannis (he also uses the German spelling Johannis) became the president, defeating long-time Prime Minster Victor Ponta. A former high school physics teacher and four-time mayor of the city of Sibiu, he is the first Romanian president to come from an ethnic minority. Iohannis is a Transylvanian Saxon, descended from the Germans who settled in Transylvania in the twelfth century—an ethnic group that was persecuted under the dictator Nicolae Ceausescu.

THE PARLIAMENT

Romania's parliament is divided into the Senate, or the upper house, and the Chamber of Deputies, or the lower house. The parliament is the sole law making authority, and members of the Parliament are elected by the people. The Romanian parliament consists of 345 deputies and 143 senators. Deputies and senators serve four-year terms. Romania's system of government is similar to the French system of government. In addition to the post of president, it also has a prime minister who heads the government. The president appoints the prime minister who, in turn, chooses the cabinet. The president can also dissolve Parliament if it fails to approve a government within sixty days.

THE PALACE OF THE PARLIAMENT

In the world of monuments, the Romanian parliament building in Bucharest is truly monumental. This huge structure, which houses both chambers of the nation's parliament, is one of the largest administrative buildings in the world, and also one of the most expensive. Construction began in 1983, during the Ceausescu regime, a time when many ordinary Romanians were starving. For that reason—as well as for its grandiose architectural style—some people consider the massive building a monstrosity. Also known as the People's Palace, it is one of Romania's top tourist destinations.

LOCAL GOVERNMENT

Romania is divided into forty-one counties, or *judete* (joo-DEH-TSE), and one municipality, Bucharest. Each county is further subdivided into towns and communes and is led by a prefect, who is appointed by the government. The prefect represents the central government at a local level. County administration is autonomous and is governed by elected county councils, who coordinate the activities of the communes and town councils in their area. Town councils and mayors are elected by the people.

THE JUDICIARY

Romania's judiciary consists of the law courts, the Ministry of Justice, and the Superior Council of Magistrates. The law courts consist of the Supreme Court, the county courts and other lower courts, as well as the military tribunals. Judges of the Supreme Court are appointed by the president to serve a six-year term. Members of the Superior Council of Magistrates are elected by the Parliament to serve four-year terms and recommend potential members of the Supreme Court to the president. The council also acts as a disciplinary court for the legal profession. The Constitutional Court was created to ensure that there is a balance of power among the various agencies within the government and that the laws passed are in line with the constitution. There are nine judges serving in the Constitutional Court. These judges serve nine-year terms and are appointed by the Parliament and the president. The Ministry of Justice consists of prosecutors who represent the general interests of society, protecting rights and freedoms and maintaining order under the law. Public prosecutors are nominated by the Superior Council of Magistrates.

INTERNET LINKS

gov.ro/en
This is the official site of the Romanian government, in English.

www.muzeulcotroceni.ro/engleza/index_eng.html
The National Cotroceni Museum site has links to other important Romanian institutions.

www.cdep.ro
The Romanian parliament, Chamber of Deputies, has information on how the Parliament works, as well as on the Palace of Parliament, with an extensive slide show. Choose English on the home page.

ECONOMY

A guide points to a vein of pyrite in a rock that contains microscopic amounts of gold at the Rosia Montana gold mine in Romania.

4

WHAT WAS ONCE A CENTRALIZED economy controlled and dictated by the Communist Party is now a free market economy. Joining the European Union in 2007 was a huge leap forward for the country. Although it is the seventeenth-largest economy in the EU, it is growing rapidly. Foreign investment is a key resource for growth, and Romania's cheap and skilled labor force, low taxes, liberal labor code, and a favorable geographical location help attract investment. Like many countries, Romania took an economic hit during the 2008—2009 global financial crisis, but has been recovering quickly. Bucharest, the capital city, is one of the largest financial and industrial centers in Eastern Europe.

An ancient gold mine in the town of Rosia Montana in northwestern Romania has been the topic of great controversy for more than a decade. A Canadian corporation wants to reopen the mine, but thousands of protesting Romanians claim it would do great harm to the environment and provide little benefit to Romania.

INDUSTRIALIZATION

Until well into the twentieth century, Romania's economy was primarily agricultural. Indeed, before World War II, it was Europe's second-largest food producer. After the war, however, Romania's leaders set about rapidly industrializing the country. Dictator Nicolae Ceausescu turned to the West for loans. This meant that the country amassed a huge foreign debt. The severity of the economic situation was made worse by a powerful earthquake in 1977, with equally disastrous floods in 1980 and 1981 that badly disrupted industrial production. Determined to pay off the huge debt quickly, Ceausescu embarked on a debt-reduction strategy that wreaked havoc on the Romanian economy and the country's people.

LEGACY OF THE PAST

The enormous economic challenges facing Romania today can only be appreciated by understanding the numerous problems inherited from the Ceausescu era. The central government in Bucharest used to set production targets for various industries without regard for the country's raw materials or resources. Large sums of money were wasted in investment schemes whose motives were for political prestige rather than economic gain or profit. For example, Ceausescu ordered the building of a canal linking Bucharest with the Danube in order to bring prestige and wealth to the capital. It was an ambitious undertaking, especially in view of the country's limited resources at that time. Meanwhile, some industries that needed an injection of capital, such as the metallurgical and chemical industries, were forced to survive with outdated equipment.

Underlying these problems was the mounting foreign debt, a result of massive loans required for the country's industrialization program. By 1981 the total debt was over $10 billion. The International Monetary Fund, the main financier, made difficult demands in return for rescheduling payments. Imports were severely reduced, especially of food, while meat continued to be exported in order to gain valuable foreign currency. This led to the rationing of meat in Romania.

In 1982, Ceausescu declared that the entire foreign debt would be paid off by 1990, and severe measures were introduced to save money. For example, bread, flour, sugar, milk, and gasoline were all rationed, with portions progressively reduced.

There was little money for purchasing new technologies, especially in the production of energy. The system for supplying gas and electricity across the country was never allowed to develop in proportion to the increase in demand. As a result, drastic measures, such as an 80 percent cut in street lighting in Bucharest from 1972 to 1989, were adopted. The law forbid office temperatures to exceed 57°F (13.8°C) even when it was below zero outside. Hot water was only available once a week. During the bitter winter of 1984, medical records show that more than thirty infants died in Bucharest's hospitals, the result of unannounced power cuts that affected their incubators. During this same time, Ceausescu was building the colossal and extraordinarily expensive Palace of the Parliament in Bucharest.

During the rationing of 1989, citizens would stand in long lines to get food for their families, such as this line for eggs in Bucharest.

PRIVATIZATION

Before the 1989 revolution there were no privately owned factories or farms. They were all owned by the state. Privatization began in 1992 with the transfer, in the form of property certificates, of 30 percent of the registered capital of state-owned commercial companies to Romanian citizens. The remaining 70 percent of businesses under state ownership were to be sold to private individuals, or companies, including foreign investors.

Romanian banks have also since been privatized. Private enterprise is also returning to the once largely state-owned industrial sector. The Romanian Development Agency was set up to encourage the growth of small-to-medium enterprises. State farms have also been broken up and returned to the families that once owned and farmed them. About 86 percent of Romania's arable land is now under private ownership.

WHERE DO PEOPLE WORK?

In 2013, Romania's labor force numbered about 9.5 million people and the unemployment rate was 7.3 percent. While the Romanian economy is improving, about 22 percent of people in Romania live below the poverty line. However, that is a great improvement over its 36 percent poverty rate in 2000. In 2014, Romania was the second poorest country in the EU, after Bulgaria.

INDUSTRY Steelworks, metallurgical complexes, machine-building, and metal-processing factories are major providers of jobs. The industrial sector employs 29 percent of Romania's labor force and provides 34 percent of the country's gross domestic product (GDP).

Factory workers produce a wide variety of products, ranging from cars to machine parts to diesel engines. In 2013, for example, some 410,997 automobiles were produced in Romania, up from 78,165 in 2000. Furniture, footwear, clothes, and textiles are also manufactured, and they compete favorably in the international market. Romania's metallurgical industry is another key industry and has a long history dating back to Roman times, when gold and silver were mined in the southwestern and western parts of the country. These metals, along with silver and aluminum, are still mined today. The metal-processing and machine-building industries account for almost one-third of the total industrial production.

FORESTRY Forests cover nearly 27 percent of Romania, giving rise to a thriving lumber industry. Hardwoods like oak and beech are used for making furniture and as building materials. Fir is used in the construction of boats and the manufacture of musical instruments.

AGRICULTURE Around 60 percent of the land is arable and farming provides about 29 percent of employment, which is a high number compared to other industrialized nations. The rich agricultural land of Romania, blessed with a suitable climate, encourages the development of cereal crops, such as wheat, corn, rye, and oats. However, this sector is not producing as much as it could be, leaving Romania to import about 70 percent of its food needs. Wine production is one of the more thriving industries, and increasing amounts

The gentle slopes of the Dealu Mare ("Big Hill") region are ideal for growing wine grapes. Here, a man surveys his vineyard.

TOURISM'S GREAT POTENTIAL

Extraordinary scenic beauty, astonishing castles and fortresses, charming medieval towns, cultural and historical treasures—Romania has all the makings of a top tourist destination. Many travelers consider it the most beautiful country in Eastern Europe. Among its top attractions are the scenic Peles Castle in Brasnov; the mysterious Bran Castle, built in 1382; the Turda Salt Mine, an extraordinary underground site dating from the Middle Ages; the colossal Palace of the Parliament in Bucharest; and the 56-mile (90 km) long Transfagarasan, a spectacular twisting mountain highway. In addition, the Danube Delta offers riverboat excursions and Black Sea beaches. Romania also boasts five World Heritage Sites.

But many potential visitors are largely unaware of Romania's natural beauty and attractions. In 2013, Romania ranked sixty-eighth in the world—and thirty-fifth in Europe—by the Travel and Tourism Competitiveness report. The rating is a significant improvement over its 2007 standing of 111th, but still shows a lack of power to reach foreign visitors.

More than 300,000 tourists visit the gardens at Peles Castle every year.

Nevertheless, tourism numbers have been climbing as the country's image has significantly improved since it threw off its communist yoke. In 2009, some 7.5 million people visited Romania, compared to 4.8 million in 2002.

Romania's tourism market remains underdeveloped, and most visitors come from neighboring countries. To become a world-class destination, Romania faces significant challenges, such as its poor infrastructure. Better roads, transportation systems, hotels, and other support systems need upgrading. For example, only 7 percent of the existing hotels in Romania are affiliated with international chains, such as Hilton or Ramada, compared to 22 percent in the EU. Another problem may be the dangerous political situation in neighboring countries—most recently Ukraine—which raises concerns about the stability of the region.

of wine are being exported. Romania is now one of the top ten wine producers in Europe, and Romanian white and red wines have won international recognition.

FISHING The rivers and lakes of Romania, and particularly the Danube Delta area and the Black Sea coastal region, support a valuable fishing industry that supplies the local and export market. Caviar, the eggs of sturgeon fish, is also an important export. Fishing is an important source of revenue and employment, but it is declining. Membership in the EU has forced Romania to comply with the EU's Common Fisheries Policy, which limits the amount of fish that can be caught. These restrictions are aimed at sustainability and address the problem of overfishing of the Black Sea. However, fishermen complain that the quotas are ruining their livelihoods.

A local fisherman pulls a fishing net into his boat in the Danube Delta.

SERVICES About 47 percent of Romanians work in the service sector, which includes the financial and business trades, hotels and restaurants, transport, and professional services. The largest employer in this sector is the retail industry, which employs about 12 percent of Romanians.

INTERNET LINKS

www.worldbank.org/en/country/romania
The World Bank's section on Romania includes interesting feature stories as well as facts and figures.

romaniatourism.com
Romania Tourism offers many photos and videos of Romania's attractions.

ENVIRONMENT

Horses Waterfall in Borsa, in the Rodnei Mountains, is the highest waterfall in Romania.

5

LIKE VIRTUALLY EVERY OTHER country on Earth, Romania has environmental issues to solve. It also has an extraordinary natural environment worth preserving. Almost half of the country is covered with natural and semi-natural ecosystems. The Danube Delta is the largest continuous marshland in Europe and supports a vast array of plant and animal life. Romania also has one of the largest areas of undisturbed forest in Europe.

NATIONAL PARKS AND PROTECTED AREAS

Romania boasts thirteen national parks, fourteen nature parks, and three United Nations Education Science and Culture Organization (UNESCO) biosphere reserves. The country has about 845 protected areas, which together make up more than 5 percent of the country's land area.

The country's first environmental protection law was passed in 1930. Over the next few years, several national parks and reserves were created, including the Retezat National Park in the Southern Carpathians and the Pietrosul Mare National Park in the Western Carpathians. The Ceahlau Massif National Park in the Eastern Carpathians has strange rock formations that have inspired many myths. The massif is said to be

The Danube is Europe's only major river which flows west to east, from Central to Eastern Europe. It flows 1,777 miles (2,860 km) from Germany's Black Forest to the Danube Delta in Romania and Ukraine, and into the Black Sea. The European Commission calls the river the "single most important non-oceanic body of water in Europe."

the home of Zamolxe, God of the Dacians, who were the ancestors of today's Romanian people.

In 1990, Romania's Danube Delta, with its unique ecological system, was designated a UNESCO biosphere reserve and a World Heritage Site. The delta is Europe's largest wetland area and has the largest reed bed in the world. It is home to a vast range of plants and animals, and is considered one of the world's most important areas for biodiversity.

FORESTS AND FORESTRY

Romania's forests cover nearly 27 percent of the country and consist mainly of deciduous hardwood trees such as beech, sycamore, maple, ash, and elm. Much of Romania's forest cover has remained untouched. Because of the remoteness of the Carpathians, the communist government did not bother to turn much of the forests into state-owned farms. At the same time, farming relied mainly on traditional methods using few chemical pesticides and fertilizers.

Two major factors are slowly changing the face of the Carpathians, especially in the lower foothills. Logging has been a major industry in Romania, and the country is one of the leading exporters of timber. This

Romanian volunteers plant fir trees in Piatra Craiului National Park in 2010. They are replacing trees that were illegally cleared.

means that many trees are felled to supply the profitable timber industry. Illegal logging is also a problem. The World Bank estimates that 5 to 20 percent of all timber cutting in Romania is illegal. The second factor is land restitution, where state land is returned to the original private owners. The Romanian government returned about 7.4 million acres (3 million hectares), or about one-third of Romania's forests, to individuals and communities whose land was seized by the communist government. According to studies, many forests have been cut down because of the absence of legislature preventing these owners from felling trees.

Chamois are large mountain goats that live in the mountains of Europe.

SURVIVAL OF THE RARE

Many of Europe's most endangered and vulnerable animals live in Romania's virgin forests and wetlands. The Romanian Carpathians are home to 6,000 brown bears, some 2,500 wolves, and 1,500 lynxes, or about 40 percent of Europe's lynx population.

The Danube Delta is home to 341 species of birds that include Europe's largest colonies of Dalmatian pelicans and Great White pelicans, as well as rare or near-extinct birds. The Danube and its tributaries teem with fish such as perch, pike, sturgeon, and carp. It's an important area for fish farming, and 135 fish species are raised there. Occasionally, small groups of Black Sea dolphins can be spotted swimming along the coast and rivers.

The poaching of Romania's animals, however, is a concern. Black Sea dolphins are often caught and sold to aquariums. World demand for caviar has resulted in the illegal fishing of sturgeon from Romania's waterways. Sturgeon fishing has been prohibited for more than a decade. Wolves are shot because of superstition and because they attack livestock. Chamois are poached for their valuable hide.

Educational programs and laws have been put in place to discourage many of these practices. However, weak enforcement and lack of government funding, as well as air and water pollution, mean that Romania's natural environment is still under threat.

POLLUTION

Air pollution in Romania is due mainly to industrial activity and urban traffic. A study from 2011 showed Bucharest to be the second most polluted capital city in Europe, after the Bulgarian city of Sofia. The study reported that intense traffic in Bucharest, along with the fact that 60 percent of the cars in the city were more than eight years old, contributed to the poor air quality.

The energy sector is a major contributor to the pollution because it relies heavily on the burning of fossil fuels. Poorer households burn low-quality coal for heat, adding to the problem.

Fortunately, the signs for the future are good. A decline in industrial activity, an increasing use of alternative power sources, and more stringent regulations have led to improvements in the quality of air over urban and industrial parts of Romania.

Headlights of the rush hour traffic light up the night in Bucharest.

ENERGY RESOURCES

Romania has large coal and oil deposits, including oil fields discovered in its section of the Black Sea in 1981. The country was once the largest oil producer in Europe, but reserves were reportedly used and wasted during the Ceausescu regime. Today, Romania has nine crude oil refineries and the fourth-largest crude oil reserves in Europe. In recent years, the government has worked to attract investment by US and other foreign oil companies in its energy resources. It's also interested in exploring development of its shale and deep-water resources, though many Romanians oppose these plans for environmental reasons.

Romania is also an important producer of natural gas, with Europe's fifth-largest natural gas reserves. Natural gases such as methane are found in the Transylvanian Plateau. Romania, however, still needs to import about 24 percent of its natural gas from Russia to meet all of its domestic power needs.

Two nuclear power plants generate about 20 percent of the country's electricity production. The country intends to build two more nuclear

THE DIRTY DANUBE

The beauty of the Danube River inspired the Austrian composer Johann Strauss to write "The Blue Danube" waltz in 1867, one of the world's best loved waltzes. Today he might call it "The Dirty Danube" and turn it into a dirge. The great river—and its tributaries—have been polluted by oil spills, toxic mine spills, industrial discharge, and bombs.

The Danube flows into the Black Sea, dumping about 1653.5 tons (1500 t) of waste into the sea each year. The river, which flows through ten countries altogether, picks up pollutants before it even reaches Romania. Agricultural runoff from farms throughout Europe drains into the river and ends up polluting the Black Sea.

In Germany and Austria, there are dozens of plastic production and processing plants on the river's banks, and plastic pollution is a serious problem which harms wildlife. In the former Soviet bloc nations, such as Hungary, communist regimes built up heavy industry along the waterway with little regard for environment. Today in western Hungary, hazardous waste in the form of toxic sludge pours into the river.

The 1990s war in neighboring Serbia contributed to the mess when bombed-out chemical and fertilizer factories spilled their toxic brew into the waters. And in Romania, in 2000, a wall collapsed at a gold mine in the northwest region of Baia Mare. The calamity released cyanide and heavy metals into the river and poisoned drinking water across the Balkans.

Despite all this, environmentalists say the situation is improving and now that eight Danube countries are part of the European Union, the EU's stiffer regulations and standards should help in the long run.

In the 1990s, the town of Copsa Mica (COPE-shah MEE-kah) in Transylvania had the dubious distinction of being "the most polluted town in Europe" and "the town where everyone is ill." The town was home to two factories, a zinc smelter and a carbon black factory, which had spewed heavy metals and black dust over the town for more than sixty years under communist rule.

The Carbosin factory produced powdered carbon used in making rubber. The black powder was released into the air and settled over the buildings, the vegetation, the people, and even the animals. All the sheep were black, and no other farm animals could stay alive in such conditions. Vegetation also died off. In fact, the entire town was so blackened by the soot that it showed up as a dark blot in satellite images.

The pollution from Sometra, a metalworks company, was less visible but more deadly. Zinc, lead, and other metals infiltrated the soil, air, and water. The soil was so toxic that even crops grown in the poisoned soil were themselves toxic. But the residents ate those vegetables because they had no choice. The authorities, who knew very well how contaminated the produce was, forbid Copsa Mica residents from selling their crops outside the town limits.

Studies found that 96 percent of the children had chronic bronchitis and respiratory problems. Two-thirds were underweight, and the rates of mental retardation and birth defects were far above average.

In the 1990s, the United Nations Industrial Development Organization undertook a seven-year project to clean up Copsa Mica. Today, although the factories have been closed and the black powder has mostly disappeared, people remain sick, suffering from lead poisoning, bronchitis, ricketts, asthma, stunted growth, depression, and alcoholism, among other illnesses. Life expectancy is nine years below the Romanian average.

plants to supply another 20 percent of its needs. The country also relies on renewable sources, mostly hydroelectric power plants, to meet its energy needs. The country is one of few in the European Union on track to meet its 2020 renewable energy target, which involves renewable energy accounting for 24 percent of Romania's gross final energy consumption.

ALTERNATIVE ENERGY

Romania relies on fossil fuels, nuclear power, and hydroelectric power to meet its domestic energy needs. To decrease the country's reliance on fossil fuels, alternative energy sources are attractive. Romania currently has thirty-eight geothermal systems that use hot water rising up from deep below the ground to heat homes and for industrial and agricultural uses.

Geothermal energy systems are especially environmentally friendly as they produce very few unhealthy byproducts and take up less space than conventional power plants. Unfortunately, as with other environmentally friendly energy systems currently in use on a small scale, geothermal usage in Romania suffers from a lack of funds and interest.

INTERNET LINKS

turism.gov.ro/wp-content/uploads/2013/05/Natura.pdf
"A Journey Into Nature," a PDF booklet published in 2011 by the Romanian Ministry of Regional Development and Tourism, has spectacular photos and information about Romania's nature reserves and wildlife.

wwf.panda.org/what_we_do/where_we_work/black_sea_basin
The WWF section on the environmental issues facing the Black Sea Basin includes the Danube Carpathian region.

www.eia.gov/countries/country-data.cfm?fips=ro
The US Energy Information Administration page on Romania has energy statistics.

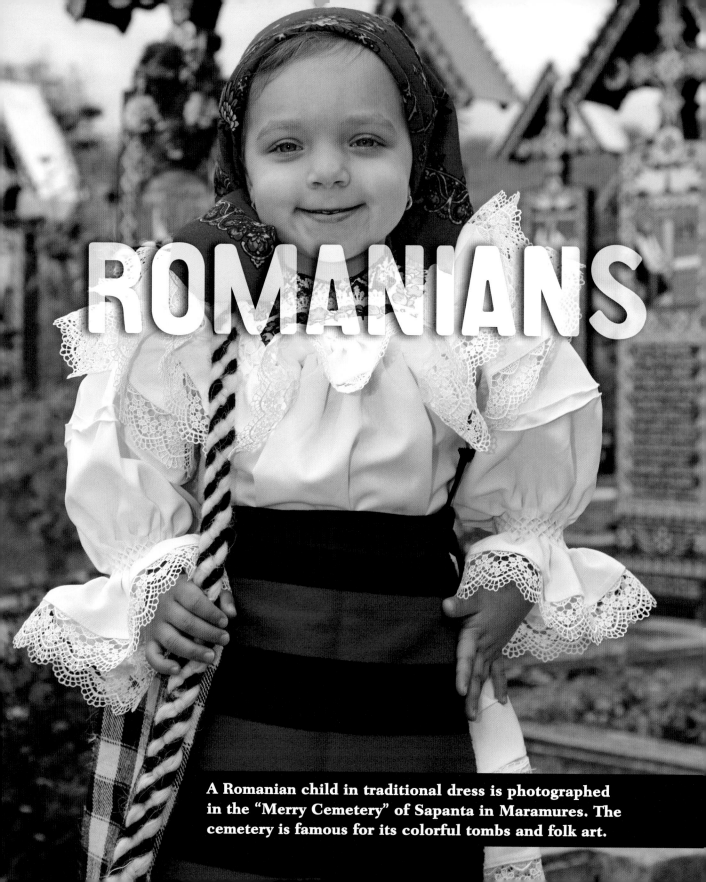

ROMANIANS

A Romanian child in traditional dress is photographed in the "Merry Cemetery" of Sapanta in Maramures. The cemetery is famous for its colorful tombs and folk art.

6

ROMANIA MEANS "LAND OF THE Romans," but much has changed in the two thousand years since the Roman Empire swept over this land. The people of Romania are not Romans, but Romanians. And who are the Romanians?

Although the Romans withdrew from this region after only two centuries, they did leave their genetic mark on the people. However, today's Romania is home to a number of other ethnicities and nationalities as well. A significant number of Hungarians live in the western part of the country, in Transylvania. Germans, also known as Saxons or Swabians, are the second most populous ethnic minority. The Roma, or Romani, a separate ethnic group of Indian origins, are found throughout the country. Some twenty other nationalities live in Romania, including Serbs, Turks, Bulgarians, Tatars, and Armenians, but their numbers are small.

THE ROMAN CONNECTION

The intermarriage of Dacians and the conquering Romans (made up of troops from Rome and other parts of the Roman Empire, such as Greece and Spain) is viewed by most modern Romanians to be their ethnic foundation. The presence of Romans in the country must have continued well beyond the formal withdrawal of Roman troops in 271 and 275 CE. Supporting evidence for this theory comes from the fact that the Romanian language—clearly Latinate in its structure—could not have evolved the way it did if the Romans completely evacuated the

In 2011, the Romanian government launched a global "Why I Love Romania" poster campaign, hailing the achievements of famous Romanians such as tennis player Ilie Nastase, gymnast Nadia Comanenci, and scientist Nicolae Paulescu, who discovered insulin.

A Transylvanian farmer uses a water buffalo, specific to the region, to assist him.

land in the third century. Archaeological evidence of coins bearing Roman inscriptions up to the fifth century has also been found. This suggests that commercial links between the Dacians and the Roman Empire continued after Roman troops withdrew.

THE QUESTION OF TRANSYLVANIA

Transylvania is historically important to both Romania and Hungary, and the issue of ownership has caused conflict between the two countries. The Hungarian name for Transylvania is Erdély (ER-day). Some Hungarians accuse the Romanian government of a campaign of ethnic cleansing to suppress the separate identity of the Hungarian minority in Transylvania. For example, Hungarian-language schools were closed down, and history books were written to correspond with the Romanian account of Transylvania's history.

Since 1989, the Romanian and Hungarian governments have worked to improve their strained relations, which began during the communist era. In 1996, Romania and Hungary signed a treaty of understanding, cooperation, and good-neighborliness. The treaty, known as the Basic Treaty, was signed at Timisoara. Hungarian-language schools have also reopened in Transylvania.

Conflicts involving Hungarians living in Transylvania are particularly significant because Romania's ethnic Hungarians form the largest minority group in Romania and are nearly 19 percent of Transylvania's population. To ensure their views are represented in Parliament, ethnic Hungarians formed their own political alliance, the Democratic Union of Hungarians in Romania (UDMR), in 1989, advocating Magyar minority rights and territorial autonomy. The group plays an active role in politics and government.

In eastern Transylvania, amid the hills and valleys of the Eastern Carpathian Mountains, lives a subgroup of Hungarian people called the Székelys. This historical region, called Székely Land, is now an ethnic enclave within Romania, with a population that is about 75 percent Hungarian—and even higher in some areas. The region has existed as a Székely district since medieval times.

After WWII, it was designated as the Magyar Autonomous Region, a semi self-governing territory, with the city of Targu-Mures as its capital. When Nicolae Ceausescu came to power, he abolished the region's autonomous status in 1968. After communism ended, Székely people hoped their autonomy would be reinstated, but it has not been.

Although many Hungarian residents have been pushing for a higher level of self governance, and many would like to have their own land, the Romanian constitution defines Romania as a "sovereign, independent, unitary, and indivisible national state." Any ethnic-based territorial autonomy, including that of the Székely Land, would appear to be unconstitutional. Nevertheless, the area is a cultural region with its own churches, museums, and tourist attractions.

SZÉKELY LAND ISSUES

- Hungarian (Székely) majority
- Romanian majority
- Roma (Gypsy) majority
- No ethnic group over 50%
- Traditional Székely Land (as of 1876)
- Proposed borders of the Székely Land as advocated by the Szekler National Council

COVASNA
Present counties of Romania

- ◉ County capitals
- ● Other towns

Sources:
1. The proposed status for the Autonomous Székely Land
2. The Romanian Census of 2002

An illegal Roma settlement shows the poverty that the people typically live in.

THE ROMA MINORITY

Despite the similarities of the names, the Roma, or Romani, people are ethnically a completely separate group from the Romanian people. Also called Gypsies, they are a migratory people who came from northern India and settled in Europe in the fourteenth century. Some Roma might have been brought as slaves by Ottoman rulers. In Walachia and Moldavia, Romani people were kept as slaves until the 1850s. After slavery was abolished, they were given Romanian citizenship. Roma have their own language, Romany, which is thought to derive from Sanskrit. Roma in Romania often speak a combination of Romany and Romanian or Hungarian.

According to the 2011 census, there are about 622,000 Roma in Romania, but many believe the true figure to be much higher. This is because some Roma do not want to be identified as Roma because of the prejudice they face. Roma are generally ostracized by Romanian society. In a 2003 Gallup poll, 31 percent of Romanians thought that Roma should not be allowed in public places such as restaurants and bars. The Roma community is very insular, living apart from society according to its own tribal rules and traditions, some of which—particularly the practice of forced child marriage—conflict with modern mores.

Roma traditionally tend to live in makeshift dwellings or shantytowns on the outskirts of big cities, especially around Bucharest. Most Roma live in poverty, and many of their homes lack basic facilities, such as electricity and water. Many are either unemployed or employed in low-paying jobs because the prejudice against them makes it difficult to obtain work. The Romanian government has taken steps to provide Roma with more opportunities to promote their culture and language. Poverty and social discrimination, however, remain the two main problems for the Roma, and they still face violence and harassment.

Prominent members of the Romanian Jewish community carry the Torah at the opening of the Holocaust memorial in Bucharest in 2009.

DISAPPEARING MINORITIES

Germans, mainly Saxons, were not granted the unrestricted right to leave Romania during the Ceausescu era. The German government campaigned for their right to leave and criticized the Romanian government's practice of granting exit permits in return for cash payments. Since the reunification of Germany and the 1989 revolution, there has been an outflow of Germans from Romania. Also in return for cash payments, the Ceausescu regime allowed Romanian Jews to leave for Israel. Before World War II, Romania was home to the third-largest community of Jews in Eastern Europe, after Poland and the Soviet Union. However, emigration, deportation, and the extermination programs carried out in Bucharest, Iasi, and other cities greatly reduced the population. Some 250,000 to 300,000 Romanian Jews were killed during the Romanian Holocaust. Today, about nine thousand to fifteen thousand Jews live in Romania, most of them in Bucharest.

TRADITIONAL COSTUME

Peasant women have traditionally made clothing by spinning, weaving, and sewing material made from wool, flax, cotton, and rough silk. The colorful embroidery work characteristic of traditional Romanian costume has also

A young farmer in traditional Romanian costume tips his hat for a photograph.

been associated with women. Men have tended to specialize in making vests, jackets, coats, and other garments from leather or sheepskin.

Basic to a woman's costume is the simple white blouse embroidered with colorful ornamentation in bright red, black, and gold. A skirt is worn over the blouse and an apron is tied at the waist with a sash. The aprons and skirts tend to feature geometric patterns woven into or embroidered on them. Scarves and veils are worn, with a long thin silk veil being reserved for special occasions. Colored headgear is popular, and regional traditions have evolved their own ways of denoting a married woman by the kind of headdress she wears.

The white blouse is also a basic item in male costume, tightened at the waist with a woolen sash or leather belt. This is usually worn with narrow, white trousers. A typical piece of headgear for men is the hat made of lambskin, black felt, or straw—depending on the time of year and the local tradition.

Over the centuries, traditional costume accommodated new materials and fashions. Today, Romanians wear typical Western clothing, but for special occasions and in less developed, rural parts of the country, traditional costume is still worn and highly regarded.

ORDINARY ROMANIANS

The typical citizen has a sense of pride in being a Romanian. In a country surrounded by more than a dozen different nationalities and races, mostly Slavic and non-Latin, Romanians take pride in their Dacian roots and long history. Pride also exists in the fact that their country has preserved its own language and religion in spite of repeated assaults on its culture by the Austro-Hungarian and Ottoman empires, and more recently by the former Soviet Union.

Romanians, especially rural Romanians, are said to be hospitable, resourceful, good-natured, and often self-critical. The simple architecture of some small rural churches and country homes, reflecting an old-fashioned modesty, is now gradually replaced by ambitious, massive, and monumental buildings—for example, some Eastern Orthodox churches.

During the 1970s and 1980s, ordinary people were brutalized by the constant struggle to survive and became progressively demoralized. Having been watched constantly by the state police for decades, many observers agree that it will take a long time for Romanians to shrug off the sense of suspicion and intense self-interest that was imposed on the otherwise warm Romanian personality. Nevertheless, it is astonishing how, in spite of having endured such harsh conditions, a sense of goodwill is preserved, especially in rural areas where the tradition of welcoming a guest is still strong.

INTERNET LINKS

www.euractiv.com/culture/hungary-romania-face-ethnic-disp-analysis-517991
"Hungary and Romania face off over an ethnic dispute" on Euractiv.com examines the Romanian—Hungarian dispute over Transylvania and Székely Land.

www.errc.org/article/being-a-gypsy-the-worst-social-stigma-in-romania/1385
An article on the European Roma Rights Centre site discusses the status of Roma people in Romania.

www.spiegel.de/international/europe/europe-failing-to-protect-roma-from-discrimination-and-poverty-a-942057.html
Spiegel Online offers an excellent and engaging article with photo gallery: "The Plight of the Roma: Europe's Unwanted People."

www.eliznik.org.uk/RomaniaPortul
"Traditional costume in Romania" has photo albums of Romanian folk clothing by region.

LIFESTYLE

Where food was once scarce, supermarkets in Romania are now well stocked with food and consumer goods.

7

THE AFTER EFFECTS OF CEAUSESCU'S bitter dictatorship continue to be felt decades after his fall. Romanians found the first decade of democracy a difficult period as they tried to cope with market forces and the removal of subsidies. They had thought their lives would improve immediately and were disappointed to discover that their standard of living got worse before it got better. But for many, it did get better, and as Romania takes great steps forward in the twenty-first century, the average Romanian's lifestyle does as well.

THE NEW ROMANIA

Where lines for bread and meat used to snake around city blocks and empty shelves were once a common sight in stores, today lines are for fast food counters and good privately baked bread. Shelves are filled with produce and meat. Supermarkets in Bucharest and other big cities stock imported items. International luxury brand stores, malls, and other modern shopping centers have sprung up in Bucharest and other

Pas Cu Pas ("Step by Step"), the autobiography of Klaus Iohannis, was a surprise best seller at an international book fair in Bucharest in November 2014. Iohannis, former mayor of the Transylvanian city of Sibiu, went on to defeat the favorite, Prime Minister Victor Ponta, in Romania's presidential election the following month.

cities, reflecting a population with the ability to purchase these goods. A new middle class has arisen that has the money to buy what was once affordable only by the rich—cars, mobile phones, imported goods. Popular cars among Romanians are made in Romania by Dacia, a subsidiary of the French auto company Renault, which bought the company in 1999. Its models are the cheapest cars in Europe, starting at around $9,100.

Computer ownership is also increasing but lags behind much of Europe. In 2011, only half of Romanians had ever used a computer, the lowest ratio in the European Union, where the average was 78 percent. Naturally, young people were far more likely to have computer skills, but they still lagged behind their European Union counterparts.

Still some old habits remain. Romanians still hoard what they can reuse—cardboard boxes, plastic bags, glass bottles. This is particularly true for many Romanians who have been left behind in the transition to a market economy, especially old-age pensioners as their pensions are low.

EDUCATION

Under communist rule, all schools were state schools run by the government. Apart from private tutors, no form of private education was allowed by law. All aspects of the curriculum were rigidly controlled by the government, but subjects like history and literature were especially prone to ideological control. There was no room for views of history that conflicted with the political system in operation within the country.

Since 1989 private educational institutions have flourished alongside public schools. Schools are widely available in cities but not in less accessible rural areas. The school attendance of children in rural areas is also much lower than in urban areas. Romania's education budget is low compared to the West—4.3 percent of gross domestic product, (GDP, which is a measure of a country's economy), compared to 5.9 percent in France, for example—which has hindered the government's ability to improve schools and school attendance, particularly in rural areas.

Education is compulsory for children up to ninth grade. Children in ninth grade graduate with a *Certificat de Capacitate,* or certificate of capacity, when

they pass their examinations. Their examination results determine what they will study in high school. About 24 percent of students go on to college.

Since the days of communist rule, many new colleges and universities have opened. Before 1989, there were fewer than twenty institutions of higher education, but today Romania has some 125 such schools. Fifty-six of these institutions are state funded. The most renowned universities are in Bucharest, Cluj, and Iasi. Medicine, law, and information technology are popular fields of study. Babes-Bolyai University in Cluj Napoca is considered Romania's top school. Romania's oldest university is the University of Bucharest, founded in 1694.

Roma children attend kindergarten in Araci, a poor village in central Romania.

WEDDINGS

Before 1989 many weddings were marked by an official ceremony at the local mayor's office followed by a simple church wedding. Since the revolution, however, there has been an increase in more elaborate traditional wedding ceremonies.

Women and children especially suffered under Ceausescu's rule because of the role they were forced to play in the government's population policy. The dictator's aim was to reach a population of thirty million by the year 2000. He believed that a country's power rested on its industrial output, and a larger workforce would mean greater production. Every woman was required by law to have at least five children, and there were tax penalties for those with fewer than three children. Married women up to the age of forty-five were subjected to compulsory monthly examinations to see if they were pregnant. If so, they were monitored to ensure they did not abort the baby.

All forms of birth control, as well as abortion, were banned for Romanian women under forty-five years old during this time, leading to the birth of thousands of unwanted children. The general lack of food and welfare services also meant that undernourished mothers gave birth to premature and underweight children. The human consequences of this, and the full horror of the government policy, only came to light after 1989 when the veil of secrecy was lifted. Romanian hospitals were full of unwanted children, as well as women suffering the effects of illegal abortions.

In 1989, after the fall of the Ceausescu regime, there were an estimated 170,000 children in Romania's orphanages. In 1990, the American television program 20/20 broadcast a documentary about one of these institutions called "Shame of a Nation." In the film, filthy, naked, skeletal children are crammed into unheated cement rooms, sitting amid their own excrement.

Upon seeing such atrocities in that and other exposes, thousands of well-meaning people in the United States and Western Europe rushed to adopt children from Romania and other former communist countries in Eastern Europe. But the adoptive parents didn't realize how deeply the effects of neglect, malnutrition, and sensory deprivation had scarred

the children. Infants raised without physical and emotional human contact tend not to develop the ability to love or return affection; they often exhibit extreme behavioral problems, and these problems can be difficult or impossible to heal.

With little regulation in post-revolution Romania, abuse of the adoption system soon became a major problem. The adoption trade also became entangled with child prostitution and organ transplant rackets. Romanian children were being sold on the Internet. In 2004, the Romanian government imposed a ban on all foreign adoptions except those by close relatives abroad. To some countries, such as the United States and Britain, the ban deprives Romanian orphans of a chance for a better life with a foreign family. The Romanian government, however, imposed the ban to align Romania with an existing European Union ban, which was introduced at the request of the EU in 2001 to protect Romania's orphans from child trafficking. The EU wants the ban to remain until Romania has tougher laws and better controls for the protection of its orphans.

Romania still has about forty thousand orphans today under the care of the government. Some of these orphans are a result of Ceausescu's population policy and some are a result of widespread poverty in Romania today.

Couples tend to marry at a later age than in the past. Before 1989, a law ensured that college graduates had to work for three years near one of the twelve largest cities in the country. This was mainly because the government wanted to control the location of the workforce and reduce the over-industrialization of large urban areas. Young graduates had little control over their immediate future, and college friends were frequently separated by being assigned to different parts of the country. This encouraged young people to marry quickly, to ensure they would be assigned together to a particular location.

In the countryside, weddings traditionally take place on a Sunday, and in some places the custom of announcing the marriage by a messenger on horseback is still observed. The bride is assisted by her maids of honor, while the best man helps the bridegroom prepare for the big event. On the day of the wedding, everyone has an appointed role: speakers at the ceremony;

Villagers in traditional dress celebrate a wedding in Gherta Mica in the Maramures region.

cooks; cup-bearers who keep the drinks flowing; musicians for pan pipes, dulcimers, and violins; and the best man, whose functions include carrying a colored pole decorated with handkerchiefs and bells during the wedding procession.

A wedding is welcome occasion for local people to parade in traditional forms of dress, including the horseman with his distinctively handwoven saddle blankets. Women attend to most of the ceremonial details, including the headdresses. Married women cover their heads with a *naframa* (NE-frah-mah), a handkerchief of silk or cotton, while unmarried females will braid their hair and leave it uncovered. The bride's hair is braided, using techniques that have been passed down from mother to daughter, and is covered with a coronet decorated with flowers, semiprecious stones, and ribbons of various colors. The bridegroom wears a felt hat covered with feathers and flowers, and by tradition he is dressed in a white vest made from the skin of a young goat, decorated with strands of colored leather. He is clean-shaven, having had his beard cut by the best man as a mark of his passing bachelorhood.

Before the day of the wedding, a special large loaf of bread is baked for the marriage ceremony. The bride and groom take bites of this loaf between them, sharing the same spoon and plate, while they are showered with grains of corn and drops of water. The showering of the couple with the basics of life—corn and water—is a symbolic blessing and a wish for them to enjoy their future life together.

HEALTH CARE

Although Romanians have universal, government-supported health care coverage, the system is apparently not working effectively. The US Embassy in Bucharest warns US travelers to Romania that medical care there is generally not up to Western standards, and basic medical supplies are limited, especially outside major cities. This is due to chronic underfunding.

Most hospitals in the country lack basic supplies, such as surgical gloves and antibiotics, forcing patients to pay for such amenities out of pocket. That means a patient entering the hospital for surgery, for example, is given a list of medical supplies, such as bandages, that they must bring with them for their operation. Such necessary supplies can add up to more money than the patient can afford. In addition, many hospital buildings are in serious need of repair and sanitation. For a country in the European Union, such conditions are considered scandalous. Those who can afford private medical care often fare better. The World Bank reports that access to health care in Romania is "skewed towards the wealthy" and that about half of poor do not seek care when needed.

Employees of the state health care system protest for more funding from the government.

Adding to the problem is the shortage of medical personnel. Although doctors and nurses are well trained, they make such low salaries—ten to fifteen times lower than in Western Europe, and lower than even the average Romanian worker's salary—that they often leave the country for better opportunities elsewhere. In 2010, the Romanian College of Physicians reported that more than four thousand doctors, or about 10 percent of the doctors in the country, had emigrated in the previous three years. The low health care salaries also invite corruption, such as the bribing of doctors, which is reportedly also a problem.

LIFE IN THE COUNTRYSIDE

Urban life in Romania has changed—and mostly improved—greatly in recent years, but life in the rural villages has been slow to catch up. In some rural areas, life seems to be caught in a time machine—many people live without electricity or even indoor plumbing. Although the people in these rural areas tend to be poor, they are also quite self-sufficient, albeit sometimes at a subsistence level. About 45 percent of Romanians live in rural areas.

In the Maramures, a remote, mountainous region on Romania's northern border with Ukraine, customs date back to ancient times. Farming traditions and practices have been passed on from earlier centuries: the use of horse-drawn plows and carriages, hand tools, and the handcrafting of life's necessities. Houses are adorned with intricate wood carvings of ropes, suns, and wolves' teeth to protect the family from harm; inside, sacred religious icons are displayed. Women may prepare food over an open fire, and often makes the family's butter and cheese by hand, because supermarkets simply don't exist. On Sundays and holidays, people often wear traditional clothing.

To visitors, the spectacular beauty of the landscapes and the charming villages, unspoiled by modern technology, can seem like a passport to medieval times. Indeed, the region is home to eight villages that have been designated as World Heritage Sites. In 2014, Britain's Prince Charles, who owns properties in Transylvania, urged Romania to preserve its rural traditions, saying they could bring in needed financial benefits through tourism. He, and others, are concerned that development will threaten the natural landscape as well as the old ways of the people. Such traditional places no longer exist in Western Europe, and could be a boon for Romania. Indeed, *National Geographic Traveler* magazine listed the Maramures area as one of the best twenty travel destinations in the world for 2015.

To many young people in rural Romania, however, poverty and backwardness can seem stifling and many leave for urban centers for education and work opportunities.

Many Romanian families tend to their land with donkeys and plows like their ancestors did.

INTERNET LINKS

www.balkaninsight.com/en/page/romania-culture-and-lifestyle-home
This section on Balkan Insight's website has interesting articles about Romanian life.

www.washingtonpost.com/sf/style/2014/01/30/a-lost-boy-finds-his-calling
"A Lost Boy Finds His Calling" is an excellent story and video from the *Washington Post* about a Romanian orphanage survivor.

www.euro.who.int/en/countries/romania
The World Health Organization has news and statistics relating to health and health care in Romania.

RELIGION

The Buna Vestire ("Annunciation") Romanian Orthodox Church in Brasov is an architectural landmark.

8

R OMANIA IS A SECULAR NATION by law, but it is an overwhelmingly Christian country in practice, with more than 90 percent of its population identifying as Christian. Most Romanians—81 percent—belong to the Eastern Orthodox Church, with small numbers of Roman Catholics, Greek Catholics, and Protestants making up the remaining Christian groups. Despite this great Christian majority, the Romanian constitution ensures freedom of religion, and small numbers of Muslims, Jews, atheists, and others also live in the nation.

The Romanian Orthodox Church is one branch of the Eastern Orthodox Church, which is a group of self-governing churches that recognizes the honorary primacy of the Patriarch of Constantinople. The role of religion in Romania has changed dramatically since the 1989 revolution.

RELIGION UNDER COMMUNISM

Romania was officially an atheist country under communist rule, although some churches were allowed to function and it was not

The eight wooden churches of Maramures were built in the seventeeth and eighteenth centuries and are UNESCO World Heritage Sites.

against the law to practice certain religions. The Orthodox Church of Romania was allowed to function as long as it cooperated with the communist government. Still, its activities were strictly supervised by the government, and active churchgoing was discouraged. For example, the communists dictated that Christmas Day was no longer a holiday but a regular working day. Some protests were organized over the years, but the authorities were always quick to put them down.

The Ceausescu regime made it clear to priests and religious authorities that they were under observation and had to accept the government's authority if they wanted to retain their positions. This situation introduced politics into religion, and priests were forced into a political role.

A number of priests—the majority, according to many Romanians—accepted the government's authority. Stories of priests colluding with the internal security police were common, and it was frequently observed that a priest could not be relied upon to keep any matter a secret from the government. In effect, some priests were accused of being spies, and since 1989 they have had the task of regaining the respect of the people.

Other priests, however, saw their role under Ceausescu quite differently. For them, their duty lay in challenging the government. The priests or religious authorities who were brave enough to challenge the government were harassed or murdered by the Securitate. The spark that ignited the revolution concerned a Romanian church leader in the Transylvanian town of Timisoara. The leader, pastor Laszlo Tokes, was being harassed by the security police, and his congregation's determination to resist his arrest by the police led to an outbreak of local resistance in Timisoara and other parts of Romania. This resistance eventually culminated in the overthrow of the government in December 1989.

RELIGIOUS PRACTICE AFTER 1989

The revolution occurred during the month of December and the Ceausescus were executed on December 25. To many people outside Eastern Europe, the idea of executing someone on Christmas Day seemed bizarre, but to many Romanians the execution and the date of the event were appropriate.

Christmas Day in 1989 was a surprisingly fine day, with a winter sun bringing a little warmth to an otherwise harsh winter. Many Romanians remember the day of the execution and the weather as having a mystical significance: the Ceausescu regime was over, and a new beginning beckoned. After the execution, the death penalty was abolished and churches were filled with worshipers, most of whom had not attended a church service for many years.

Today, the Romanian constitution guarantees religious freedom, and the Romanian government generally respects the people's rights to practice any religion they choose. But the country's laws give the government a strong say over religious life. For instance, the government can prohibit certain religious organizations from operating within Romania.

EASTERN ORTHODOXY

Eastern Orthodoxy is the branch of Christianity that follows the faith and practices defined by the universal church. It regards itself as the one, original Church established by Saint Paul and the Apostles, and its faith as the true continuation of the faith founded by Jesus Christ. (Other Christian churches make the same claim.) The term "universal," meaning "one" or "whole," applies to the Catholic Church before the split between the Western and Eastern churches in the year 1054. The word "orthodox" means, essentially, "true faith."

The reasons for the split of the universal church are numerous and complicated. They are related to the division of the Roman Empire into an eastern and western half, centered in the cities of Constantinople (present-day Istanbul) and Rome respectively.

Originally the entire Christian church worked together to establish a consensus on matters of doctrine. However, the two branches of Christianity evolved in different directions because of the culture and philosophy of the lands in which they developed. The Western church, which developed in Rome and parts of Western Europe, leaned toward a more legalistic approach, while Eastern Christianity, which developed in Greece, the Middle East, Eastern Europe, Russia, and northern Africa, espoused a more mystical theology. During the ninth century, conflict involving differences of opinion over doctrinal matters widened, leading to the Great Schism of 1054. This is considered to be the start of the division between the two churches. By the 1450s, when Constantinople fell to the Muslim Turks, the split was permanent.

ORTHODOX BELIEFS

The Eastern Orthodox Church (also referred to as the Byzantine Church), like Protestantism, rejects the belief that the pope is infallible. Roman Catholics believe that when it comes to theological matters, the pope cannot make a mistake. There are also other areas where the two branches of the Catholic Church disagree. However, on other essential matters, the Orthodox Church shares many basic tenets of faith with the Roman Catholic Church, including these:

TRINITY The Holy Trinity is the idea that God is one indivisible god made up of three distinct divine "persons"—the Father, the Son, and the Holy Spirit. Understanding the nature of the Trinity is understood to be a mystery, beyond human comprehension, and accessible only through spiritual experience.

RESURRECTION OF CHRIST The life, death, and resurrection (coming back to life after death) of Jesus Christ are understood to be real, historic events as described in the gospels of the New Testament. Jesus is seen as the Son of God, both human and divine.

TRANSUBSTANTIATION This is the belief that in the celebration of the Eucharist, or Holy Communion, ordinary bread and wine are literally—not just symbolically—transformed into the body and blood of Christ.

AFTERLIFE After a person dies, the soul is separated from the body and resides in either Paradise (Heaven) or Hades (Hell). Unlike Roman Catholicism, the Orthodox Church does not accept the concept of Purgatory, a transitional state between the two. Both Churches believe that the soul and body will be reunited at the time of the Final Judgment.

ICONS

The Romanian Orthodox Church, in common with all Eastern Orthodox churches, places great importance on icons, or holy images. Usually these are flat panel paintings illuminated by candles. An icon is traditionally regarded as a kind of window between the earthly and the spiritual worlds; a window through which an inhabitant of the celestial world—a saint, or Christ himself—looks into the human world. The image recorded in the icon is a sacred one because of the belief that the true features of the heavenly spirit have somehow been imprinted in a two-dimensional way on the icon.

The Merry Cemetery of Sapanta, Maramures, has elaborately decorated headstones that depict the life of the dearly departed with poems and images.

In Western churches, it is customary for worshipers to sit or kneel while attending a church service. In the Eastern Orthodox tradition, worshipers stand to pray with their arms at the sides, except when making the sign of the cross. The commandment to stand is explicitly stated in the liturgy. Before the reading of the Gospel, the priest cries out, "Wisdom! Let us stand erect."

The clasping of hands in prayer is not a gesture found in the Eastern Orthodox Church. Instead there is a gamut of different gestures: making the sign of the cross with three fingers, bowing with arms dangling, kneeling, touching the floor with the hands, and sometimes lying prostrate on the floor, with arms outstretched and the forehead pressed against the floor.

This belief in the sacred nature of an icon was developed by early religious scholars in the eighth and ninth centuries into the concept of incarnation, meaning that God appears in human form. The idea was that Christ becomes incarnate in the very materials of the icon—the wood, plaster, paint, and oils. The veneration shown to an icon is not worship of the object itself, but rather of the divine image as glorified by the object. That understanding helps to explain the extraordinary reverence accorded to icons in the religion.

A believer goes up to the *iconostasis*—the wall of paintings that separates the sanctuary from the nave—and kisses the icons. On the feast day of a particular saint, the icon of that saint is displayed on the lectern where the faithful pay their respects by a kiss and a bow, and then make the sign of the cross before rejoining the congregation.

At home, a Romanian Orthodox family usually has an icon hanging in the eastern corner of the living room and another in the bedroom. Traditionally, a guest on entering a room first greets the icon by making the sign of the cross and bowing to it.

Icons have a curious archaic strangeness that often makes them appear mysterious even to the nonbeliever. As a form of art, icons have no concept of authorship. This is one of the differences between the art of the icon and the art of Western Christianity. For centuries, the Eastern Orthodox Church has been content to repeat certain types of sacred images. The craft of producing icons was done in monasteries, with a group of monks working together on one icon. One monk might work on the eyes or hair, while another would devote himself to painting the robes of the figure being represented. Icon painters (iconographers) prepared themselves for painting through fasting, prayer, and Holy Communion, because it was believed that to paint Christ better, one must have a close relationship with God. Today, some iconographers are specially trained laypeople.

During the eighth and ninth centuries, partly through the influence of Islam, an opposition to images in worship began to pervade the Eastern Orthodox Church. During the annual Feast of Orthodoxy, instituted in 842 CE, the entire Orthodox Church celebrates and honors the victory of those who supported the use of icons during worship over the iconoclasts, who opposed the use of icons.

The iconostasis in the Cathedral of Curtea de Arges gleams with gold.

A belief in vampires, or strigoi, *existed in Romania and neighboring parts of Southeastern Europe long before the Dracula story appeared at the end of the nineteenth century. In fact, the strigoi has its roots in ancient Dacian mythology.*

Vampirism is related to the notion that the soul may not always leave a person's body after death. A vampire is a corpse that remains undead because its spirit still resides in the body, which does not decompose, no matter how long it has been buried in the ground. One reason this might occur would be if a person dies in an obvious state of sin—a death by suicide, for example. In that case, the soul is supposedly unable to leave the body in the normal way. Romanians used to particularly fear death through hanging because of the notion that constriction of the neck forced the soul downward and hence prevented its escape from the body. It is a custom to cover mirrors in the home of the recently deceased, in case the departing spirit becomes trapped upon seeing its reflection.

This shadow of a vampire is a scene from the film classic *Nosferatu*.

Vampires are feared because they are thought to return at night to the village and the homes where they once lived. Unchristened babies are thought to be vulnerable because they could be made into vampires. Two nights of the year are especially prone to vampire visitations: St. George's Day (April 23) and the night before St. Andrew's Day (November 29). Offerings of food and drink must be made available on those days, and garlic helps to repel vampires. The idea of the vampire biting the neck of its victim and sucking blood is partly a literary invention; in Romanian folklore, a touch, or even a glance, from a vampire is enough to bring about death.

Various stories have tried to explain the belief in vampires. For example, in the past, cases of premature burials were common because there was no sure way of determining death, hence the existence of the living "dead." What is evident is that the belief in vampirism has been a part of Romanian folklore for many centuries, and a willingness to accept the idea can still be found among the more superstitious people in the countryside.

In Romanian Roma folklore, it is believed that vampires can also function during part of the day, exactly at midday when there is no shadow cast by the sun. For that short duration, Roma consider it unsafe to travel out in the open because the vampire influence is potently present and poses a threat to ordinary mortals. Roma also believe that only a vampire corpse of their own undead can threaten them; the vampires of non-Roma ignore them and can in turn be ignored.

Like the vampire phenomenon, a belief in werewolves was long part of traditional Romanian folklore. It was once a common notion throughout Europe, but has largely died out and, unlike vampirism, has virtually no hold upon the imagination of even superstitious Romanians. Rational explanations for werewolves include the medical condition of lycanthropy (an unreasonable and obsessive belief that one is a wolf); the rare disease of erythropoietic porphyria, which results in inflamed and itchy skin after short exposures to sunlight; and hirsutism, which causes the sufferer to develop excessive growth of body and facial hair.

INTERNET LINKS

patriarhia.ro/en
The Romanian Orthodox Church, official site of the Romanian Patriarchate is available in English, and includes a detailed history of the Church.

christianity.about.com/od/easternorthodoxy/a/orthodoxbeliefs.htm
About Religion, "Eastern Orthodox Church Beliefs and Practices," and other articles are clear and informative.

www.bbc.com/news/magazine-23420668
BBC News Magazine's "Romania's costly passion for building churches" includes information about the new cathedral in Bucharest.

www.rofmag.com/folkroots/vampires-in-folklore-and-literature/
Realms of Fantasy, "Folkroots: Vampires in Folklore and Literature" is an intelligent article that includes Romanian folklore.

LANGUAGE

A newsstand in Bucharest offers plenty of reading material.

9

ROMANIAN IS A ROMANCE LANGUAGE, but that doesn't mean it's the language of love. The Romance languages—Spanish, Portuguese, French, Italian, Romanian, and Catalan—are a group of modern languages that evolved from spoken, or vernacular, Latin between the sixth and ninth centuries and spread across parts of Europe. This language group is also sometimes called the Latin languages. The term "Romance" in this case means "Roman," and the language of the Romans in those days was a vernacular, or informal, Latin. The "Roman" language came to Romania the same way the nation's name did—by way of the Roman conquerors during the years of the Roman Empire.

People who are fluent in Italian and French are able to understand many words and phrases in Romanian, even though the language has also been influenced by non-Romance tongues such as Greek, Turkish, Hungarian,

In written Romanian, the name of months and days of the week are not capitalized as they are in English. For example, the first month of the year is *januarie* (ya-nwa-rye), and the first day of the work week is *luni* (loon). Even the name of the language itself, Romanian, is lower cased: *limba română*.

and Slavonic. Educated Romanians speak English, French, and German as well as Romanian. The chief minority language is Magyar, the language of ethnic Hungarians. Other languages spoken include German, Romany, Serbian, Ukrainian, Slovak, Czech, Bulgarian, and Turkish. National television and radio broadcasts are made in Hungarian and German during set periods of each day.

Romanian Words and Phrases		
English	**Romanian**	**Pronunciation**
Hello	Bună ziua	BOO-nuh ZEE-wah
How are you?	Ce mai faci?	chay my FAHtch
I'm fine, thanks	Bine, mulţumesc.	BEE-nay, MOOL-tsoo-mesk
My name is ...	Mă numesc	mah noo-MESK
What is your name?	Cum vă numiti?	koom vuh noo-MITS?
Yes	Da	DA
No	Nu	NOO
Please	Poftiti	POF-teets
Good morning	Buna dimineata	BOON-a di-mi-nee-AT-sa
Goodnight	Noapte bună	nop-tay BOON-a
Goodbye	La revedere	la rev-eh-DE-ray
I love you.	Te iubesc.	tay yoo-BESK.

ROMANIAN LANGUAGE

As in most tongues, the language did not remain static over the centuries, but changed and evolved to reflect the history of its people. While the structure of the language is clearly Latinate, some words have Slavic, Turkish, and Hungarian origins. These influences reflect the political history of Romania.

Romanian nouns have three genders: masculine, feminine, and neuter. The plural of nouns usually ends in "—i," "—uri," or "—e," as in *case* (CAH-se; "houses"), and *copaci* (CO-PAH-CHI; "trees"). Adjectives are usually placed after the word they describe, and pronouns change their form slightly to agree with the gender of the noun.

The usual rule for pronunciation is that all letters are pronounced. The word for food is *mincare* and it is pronounced mahn-KHAR-ay. When words end in consonants, the stress falls mostly on the last syllable. Unlike the English language, two vowels coming together are pronounced separately and do not combine to form new sounds.

LANGUAGE ISSUES

Romanian is the official language of Romania and is spoken by about 89 percent of the people. About 7 percent speak Hungarian and 1.5 percent speak German. Romanian laws include linguistic rights for all minority groups that form more than 20 percent of a population in any given locality. This includes the adoption of signage in minority languages, access to local administration and justice systems in their mother tongue, the right to receive education in that language, and a series of other rights.

The Kilometer Zero of Freedom and Democracy monument in Bucharest is a memorial to those who died in the 1989 revolution.

It hasn't always been this way, though. Before 1989, the Communist Party was committed to a policy of Romanization. Bilingual inscriptions on public buildings were replaced with Romanian texts, and in one Transylvanian town, Cluj-Napoca, the Latin inscription on a monument to the Hungarian King Matyas was replaced with a Romanian one. Some Hungarian young people demonstrated, and the police were called in.

In the Ceausescu era, minority-language education and literature were severely restricted. A Hungarian-language university in Transylvania to provide higher education for ethnic Hungarians in Romania was closed down in 1959 during the communist regime.

Romany is not taught in many schools, but it is at this one in Bucharest.

German, which is spoken in parts of western Romania, was also restricted, as was Romany, the language of the Roma. Today, more Romanians, and not just those of German descent, are learning German so that they can do business with people in other parts of Europe.

English has also become a popular second language, particularly among young people. As a result, English loan words, such as *week-end*, *interviu* ("interview"), *fotbal* ("football" meaning soccer), and *sandvia* ("sandwich"), are creeping into the Romanian language.

A MIXTURE OF LANGUAGES

In the capital of Bucharest and in some other towns, it is common to hear German, Bulgarian, Turkish, or Serbian being spoken. Over the centuries, a number of words have entered the Romanian language from other cultures—the word *bai* (baa-I), for example, meaning "trouble," is a Hungarian word, as is *hotar* (ho-TAR), which means "border."

Hungarian is a unique language, classified as a member of the Finno-Ugric family of languages, bearing little in common with any other language. Its nearest linguistic relative is Finnish, but for all practical purposes the two languages are quite distinct. Hungarian is regarded as a difficult language to learn. It is an agglutinating language, which means its vocabulary arises from a number of root words that are modified and altered to express different ideas and shades of meaning.

Slavic words make up between 5 percent and 10 percent of Romanian vocabulary. There are also Albanian and Greek influences. The centuries during which Romania came under the influence of the Turkish empire has also left its mark on the Romanian language. An example of a Turkish word is *bacsis* (baak-SHISH) meaning "tip," as in tipping a waiter.

The Roma of Romania also have their own language, Romany, which until recently had no tradition of writing. The first Romanian—Romany dictionary appeared after 1989. Despite the similarity of the names, there is no connection between the Romanian and Romany languages.

Romanian cookbooks, some of them translations of English language cookbooks, are for sale at a bookstore.

INTERNET LINKS

www.omniglot.com/writing/romanian.htm
Omniglot's page on the Romanian language includes the alphabet, pronunciation guides, many useful phrases with audio samples, and many links.

romaniatourism.com/romanian-language.html
This site's Romanian language page has many helpful phrases and pronunciations.

ARTS

Painstakingly hand-painted Easter eggs are an Eastern European tradition, and very popular in Romania.

10

THE ARTS OF ROMANIA ARE AS old as time and as new as today—from the Dacian fortresses of the Orastie Mountains, dating from the first millennium BCE to the latest movie from a "new wave" Romanian film director. More than in some cultures, the folk arts of this country continue to thrive, not just as nostalgia but as the daily expression of the people, particularly in rural areas. The impressive visual arts range from frescos in centuries-old buildings, paintings, and sculpture, to traditional works such as carvings, crafts, elaborately embroidered costumes, and skillfully woven carpets. But the aftermath of the restrictive communist era has spurred an upsurge of theater, dance, music, and film as well.

Peles Castle, in Sinaia, is a relatively new castle, completed in 1883, compared to many others in Romania that date to the Middle Ages. It was the first castle in Europe to be entirely lit by electric light, and in 1906, it became the first place in Romania to show a movie.

CLASSICAL MUSIC

During the years of communist rule, Western music—pop, rock, jazz, and such—was frowned on, if not banned. Classical music, a genre of European origin, was provided with generous state sponsorship, which meant each major town had at least one philharmonic orchestra or opera house, and it ensured that ticket prices were affordable for ordinary people.

After 1989, subsidies were withdrawn, making it difficult for many companies to survive, as the cost of running an orchestra is quite high. However, the new attitude of freedom allowed people to embrace popular music of all kinds. One has only to view the long list of music festivals held each year to see the enthusiasm for jazz, electronica, rock, pop, and more.

Soprano Angela Gheorghiu is a well-known Romanian opera star.

Romantic composer George Enescu (JHOR-jeh en-ES-coo) (1881—1955) is one of Romania's greatest musicians and his influence is still felt in Romania. Enescu was a composer, violinist, pianist, and conductor of world fame. He is well known for integrating themes of peasant folk music into his own classical compositions, and his "Romanian Rhapsodies" is noted for its haunting traditional melodies of rural Romanian music. Enescu was a highly respected violin teacher. The American violinist Yehudi Menuhin was one of his outstanding pupils. Another world-renowned Romanian musician is the late Munich Philharmonic conductor Sergiu Celibidache (1912—1996). Angela Gheorghiu (1965—) is Romania's top opera singer, acclaimed around the world. She is also a fierce ambassador for Romania and its culture.

FOLK MUSIC

Folk music is the strongest and richest form of music in the country and is among the most enduring and fruitful traditions of folk music in Europe. A diversity of styles that stretch back centuries have been passed down and improvised from one generation to the next. Only in the last thirty years or so has a sustained effort been made to record this rich heritage.

Folk music is still part of the living culture of the people and is enjoyed at weddings, funerals, and various festivities where dance and music are customary. Different regions of the country evolved their own special forms, for example, *doina* (doi-NAH) music is associated with Maramures in the northwest of the country. Doina music has been compared with American blues because of its soulful and melancholy rhythms. In the more mountainous parts of the country, the music tends to relate to the working lives of the shepherds, and is played on folk instruments such as panpipes and the *buchium* (BOO-chium), a long wooden wind instrument rather like an alpenhorn. Gheorghe Zamfir (1941—), known as the "King of the Pan Flute," has made many recordings, and his music has been used in a number of movie soundtracks.

Gheorghe Zamfir performs with his panpipes.

TRANSYLVANIAN MUSIC

The mix of ethnic Romanians and Hungarians in Transylvania has made the region particularly rich in folk music. When Hungary was occupied by the Ottoman Turks for 150 years, Transylvania remained an independent principality with its cultural identity intact. In the early twentieth century, the famous Hungarian composer Béla Bartok (1881—1945) went there in search of the Asiatic roots of his country's music, which had been lost in Hungary itself. The old village settlement patterns survived, and the lack of contact with the outside world during the Ceausescu period helped to preserve the region's unique musical heritage and traditions.

Transylvania, however, is not a mere enclave for Hungarian music. It is a unique blend of different traditions. It is not the same as Hungarian music in

MUSIC OF THE MOUNTAINS

Such is the richness of Romanian folk music that there are small pockets of the country that preserve their own unique musical heritage. A remarkable example of this is the area known as Ghimes, a mountainous pastoral area between Moldavia and Transylvania. Ethnic Hungarians live here, having migrated across

the mountains many centuries ago, and their music is heard nowhere else in the country. It has a wild and reckless sound that outsiders associate with gypsies and is played on just two instruments: a violin and a gardon *(gar-DON), the latter being shaped like a cello but played in the manner of a percussion instrument, with the strings being hit by a small stick.*

Hungary or Romanian music in the rest of Romania, but only a trained ear can differentiate the melodies and rhythms of the two cultures. The typical Transylvanian ensemble is a string trio: a viola, a double bass, and a violin that is modified to amplify the sound of the ordinary instrument. Such bands frequently play at weddings and they need to be heard above the loud noise of the festivities. Sometimes another violinist joins the band to add volume and contribute to a fuller sound. The *kontra*, an instrument similar to the viola but with only three strings and a flat bridge that enables chords to be played, is often used in the ensemble, and it gives Transylvanian music its distinctive sound.

Most of the folk musicians are Roma, who have a rich music tradition of their own. In Transylvania, the Roma have created a distinct musical form combining Hungarian, Romanian, and Roma melodies.

LITERATURE

As far back as the fourteenth century in Romania, monks would copy religious manuscripts, usually in Slavonic. The Romanian language came into use in the mid-sixteenth century, but it was only in 1860, when Romania officially switched to the Latin alphabet from the Cyrillic version, that modern Romanian literature was born.

Some of Romania's most famous nineteenth-century writers and poets include Vasile Alecsandri, Ion Creanga, Mihai Eminescu, and I. L. Caragiale. Creanga is known for his humorous stories. His most important work is *Amintiri din Copilarie* (*Childhood Memories*). Probably the best-known Romanian poet is Eminescu, who died at age thirty-nine from ill health. Some of his more famous poems include "Luceafarul" (translated as "Evening Star," "Lucifer," or "Hyperion") and "Scrisorile" ("Epistles"). Marin Preda is one of the more well-known post-World War II writers. He is known for his award-winning novel *The Great Lonely One* (1972). Marin Sorescu is also a famous poet and dramatist.

A trend that emerged after 1989 is that of the documentary literature, which detail events over a period of time. One of the most famous in this genre is *The Silent Escape: Three Thousand Days in Romanian Prisons* by Lena Constante. It is a first-person account of the author's twelve years of solitary confinement in a Romanian prison—the longest by any woman in Romania—after she was charged falsely with espionage.

Sihastria Monastery in Moldavia is one of the famous painted monasteries.

PAINTED MONASTERIES

The region of northeastern Romania has a number of medieval monasteries with painted exterior walls. The wall paintings, like the monasteries, date from the fifteenth and sixteenth centuries, and were a way of communicating church dogma and history to the illiterate peasants. The paintings vividly

DRACULA—PURE FICTION?

More than any other work of literature, the novel Dracula, *written in 1897, has come to be associated with Romania. But its author Bram Stoker was Irish, not Romanian, and in fact had never been to Transylvania, where part of his story is set.*

In this Gothic horror tale, Count Dracula is a shape-shifting vampire living in a castle in the Carpathian Mountains of Transylvania. Dracula travels to England to find new blood and to spread the curse of the undead. While there, he takes the form of a wolf and kills several people before being forced to return to Transylvania.

The book became hugely popular in Europe and the United States and spawned many movies. The first, the German movie Nosferatu *(1922), is considered a film classic; when it came out it only heightened the public's interest in Dracula. The 1931 Hollywood movie* Dracula *starred Hungarian-American actor Bela Lugosi, seen below, as Count Dracula. His portrayal, with black cape and thick Hungarian accent, is still seen as the definitive depiction of the vampire count.*

The Dracula story draws many tourists to Romania, and there are attractions there to lure them. Bran Castle near Brasov is popularly known as "Dracula's Castle" and certainly looks the part, although there is no actual connection. But many Romanians regret that their country is associated with an Irishman's horror myth and wish that other, more positive aspects of their arts and culture could elicit such international fascination.

illustrate both the punishments for sinners and the rewards due to the faithful in the next world; as such, they taught the peasants to obey and fear their spiritual and political masters. However, the quality of the artwork goes beyond mere propaganda, and the range of the images is both startling and sophisticated. Today they are regarded as masterpieces of Byzantine art, and seven of the churches have been designated as UNESCO World Heritage Sites.

The spiritual architect of the painted monasteries was voivode Stephen the Great, a celebrated military commander under whose rule, from 1457 to 1504, a number of monasteries and churches were built. The exterior frescos represent one of the most precious examples of medieval art: biblical tableaux recording the fears and aspirations of society in the Middle Ages.

ROMANIAN ARTISTS

Eugène Ionesco, born in Romania in 1912, was educated in Bucharest and Paris, where he settled prior to World War II. He is most famous for his one-act plays that are characteristic examples of surrealist theater. Having spent so much of his life in Paris, he is often regarded more as a French artist than a Romanian one. Similarly, the poet Tristan Tzara (1896–1963) was born in Romania but spent most of his life outside the country. Despite this, both these surrealist artists show, in their rejection of realism and logic, an affinity with the unreal and mysterious world of the traditional Romanian folktale.

The work of the poet Mihai Eminescu (1850–1889), on the other hand, is regarded as the epitome of the Romanian soul in its more idealistic mood. Influenced by the European Romantics, his poetry extols the virtue of solitary reflection and stoicism by an individual when faced with disappointment and failure in personal, and especially romantic, life. Even though 1989 was the centenary of his death, the event was passed over with little notice—typical of the way in which the communist regime prevented any individual, apart from Ceausescu himself, from enjoying too much fame. In 1990, a year after the revolution, far more effort went into recognizing the country's most respected poet.

In the field of sculpture, the Romanian Constantin Brancusi (1876–1957) is world famous. He was a carpenter's apprentice before leaving to study at

This monastery, built in 1488 by Stephen the Great, is probably the most famous of the painted churches and is sometimes called "the Sistine Chapel of the East" after the renowned, Michelangelo-painted chapel in Rome. Voronet's wide expanse of paintings covers both the interior and exterior of the building. In particular, its fresco "The Last Judgment" is generally considered the finest example of Romanian church

art. The central figure of Christ sits above a chair that has the Latin inscription meaning "Toll Gates of the Air," where the recently deceased are judged and sent to their final destinations. By the side of Christ are painted a whole host of figures: Adam and Eve,

Moses, martyrs, and the prophets. On each side of the deceased are the souls who are doomed to hell, recognizable by their turbans and tall hats. They were depicted as the Turks and Tatars, who were the very real enemies of Moldavia in the fifteenth century. Farther down, two angels are seen blowing on the buchium, a long wind instrument, which is a signal for graves to open and wild animals to appear bearing the remains of the bodies they have devoured.

The various symbolic images would have resonated with meaning for a fifteenth-century audience. Many of the frescos are painted in an intense shade of blue that is so distinctive it has been given the name of Voronet blue. The composition of the paint continues to remain a mystery more than five hundred years after the church was built.

the Bucharest Academy. In 1904, he left for Paris on foot, having insufficient money to travel, and he lived in the French capital for the rest of his life. He turned down an invitation to join Auguste Rodin's studio, although the influence of Rodin is apparent in his "Sleeping Muse" of 1910, the first of many characteristic, highly polished, egg-shaped sculptures. He worked with stone, marble, steel, and wood, and many of his highly regarded works are on display in museums in the United States and France. Brancusi was born in the countryside and spent part of his young life as a shepherd. His love for nature is clear in his art, in which he fuses natural forms with the themes of modern art.

"The Table of Silence," a stone sculpture ,made by Constantin Brancusi, is in Targu Jiu, Romania.

FOLK ART

Present-day Romanian folk art is mainly confined to the northwest region of Maramures. In fairly remote villages, the residents have retained features of their culture and lifestyle that have not changed for centuries. It is one of the few parts of Europe where some people still wear traditional clothing daily

A treasured folk art tradition in Romania, as well as throughout Eastern Europe, is the art of the painted egg. In Romania, they are called oua incondeiate ("painted eggs"), but in the United States they are more commonly known as Ukrainian Easter eggs or pysanky. Since Easter is the most important day in the Orthodox Christian calendar, and eggs are symbolically linked to Easter, these little art objects are usually made at that time, traditionally by women and children. Today the eggs are also offered for sale year-round, typically to tourists.

The process is complicated and takes may steps. The finished eggs, often decorated with intricate designs, are beautiful but fragile. The designs, symbols, and colors vary from country to country, but the procedure is much the same.

Starting with a blown-out white eggshell, the artist applies colors in a batik, or wax-resist, process working from light to dark. Using an instrument called a stylus, which resembles a tiny metal funnel attached to the end of a small stick, the artist scoops up molten beeswax from a pan on a hotplate or stove. The wax flows through the tiny hole in the funnel like ink onto the egg's surface. First the painter covers all areas with wax that are to be white in the final design. The egg is then placed in a dye bath—yellow, perhaps—and the shell takes the color everywhere except

under the wax. When that color dries, the artist draws more melted wax on the areas to remain yellow. The layers continue to the darkest dye bath, often black. At that point, the egg painter gently melts all the wax off the egg, usually by holding it to a candle flame, and the shell reveals its multi-colored design. The wax also leaves a sheen on the egg, adding to its beauty.

and where their adherence to the Eastern Orthodox Church is mingled with a far older paganism that is expressed in a belief in spiritualism.

One of the most impressive folk crafts is the elaborate woodwork adorning village buildings. Doorways and windows of homes are carefully carved with decorative motifs, and the entry to a farmhouse is enhanced by an elaborately carved wooden gateway, which historically displayed a family's community status. Beautiful and intricate carvings are also found in the woodcraft of the eighteenth-century wooden churches scattered across rural Romania. Hungarians and Germans living in Romania also have their own folk art traditions and costumes.

A Romanian man creates his wares from wood in the traditional way.

FOLKTALES AND BALLADS

The writer Ion Creanga (1837–1889) is little known outside of Romania, where he is renowned as a storyteller and folkloric writer. *Childhood Memories* is his most famous book, and in it he recalls his own childhood when folk ballads were an important influence. Creanga himself employed the language and imagery of traditional folktales in his fiction, and his work evokes the peculiar nature of a folk art that has now virtually disappeared from Europe.

Popular ballads flourished in Romania between the sixteenth and nineteenth centuries and were told to the accompaniment of music on a lute, a zither, or a *cimpoi* (CHIM-poy), an instrument resembling a bagpipe. Although the vocabulary is quite simple, the ballads are full of verbal rhymes, metaphors, and the personification of natural forms, such as an oak tree or a bird. Such ballads evoke a world where the bond between people and nature was far closer than it is today.

FILMS

The potential of cinema as an art form was quickly recognized in Romania. In the early decades of the last century, Bucharest was one of the film centers of Eastern Europe, and many artists turned to the cinema as their preferred art form.

The Romanian animator Ion Popescu-Gopo won a major award at the 1957 Cannes Film Festival for a short animated film called *Brief History*. The story linked the traditional folktales of Romania with the new form of the cinema.

The allegorical approach was developed in a different direction in the late 1970s due to the repressive censorship system in the country. Film directors were forced to conceal their dissident mood under the guise of film parables. These could be decoded by an audience who understood the social and political meaning behind various innocent-looking images. Such films became known as iceberg movies because their true meaning lay hidden and what was seen was only a small part of the message.

The fall of communism and the transition period has provided Romanian moviemakers with much material. Lucian Pintilie is a renowned Romanian director whose works have been shown at the prestigious Cannes Festival in France. His 1992 film *The Oak* deals with life under Ceausescu, while his 2003 film *Niki et Flo* dramatizes the attitudes of post-1989 Romanians toward their country, emigration to the United States, family, and aging. Another award-winning film is *Occident* (2002) by Cristian Mungiu that also discusses life after 1989 and Romanians' desire to seek a better life in the West.

So many new Romanian filmmakers burst out in the twenty-first century that some observers have declared the trend the "Romanian New Wave." Some of the most acclaimed films and their directors from this group include *The Death of Mr. Lazarescu* (2005) by Cristi Puiu; *4 Months, 3 Weeks, and 2 Days* (2007) by Cristian Mungiu; *12:08 East of Bucharest* (2006), by Corneliu Porumboiu; and *Child's Pose* (2013) by Calin Peter Netzer.

INTERNET LINKS

romaniatourism.com/arts.html
This tourism site offers a nice overview of Romanian arts and crafts with photos and links to art museums.

romaniatourism.com/painted-monasteries.html
The Painted Monasteries of Bucovina can be found here.

whc.unesco.org/en/statesparties/ro
The Romanian properties on UNESCO's World Heritage List, as well as many other notable sites, can be accessed from this page.

theculturetrip.com/europe/romania/articles/the-legends-of-romanian-music-classical-sounds-and-jazz-rhythms/
"The Legends of Romanian Music: Classical Sounds and Jazz Rhythms" highlights some Romanian music stars.

www.romanianvoice.com/poezii/poeti_tr/eminescu_eng.php
Read the poems of Mihai Eminescu in English on this page of Romanian Voice. The website itself offers a large selection of poetry, short stories, folktales, and much more, but only a few are available in English.

www.nytimes.com/2008/01/20/magazine/20Romanian-t.html
"New Wave on the Black Sea" is an in-depth article from the *New York Times* magazine about the new wave of Romanian film directors.

LEISURE

Dazzling the crowds at the 1976 Olympics, Nadia Comaneci scores an unheard of perfect score.

11

PEOPLE WORK HARD, WHETHER IN the cities or the country, so there isn't a huge amount of time for leisure. What time there is might be spent going for a walk in a park or having a family picnic. Romanians also enjoy a game of chess, listening to music, and going to the movies.

Larger cities offer many diversions, from shopping to museums to night life, much like most modern cities anywhere. Throughout Romania, mobile phone and Internet access is excellent. In 2013, Romania ranked fifth in the world and second in Europe on Internet connection speed.

Romanian Simona Halep is a rising star in the world tennis scene.

TAKING IT EASY, RURAL STYLE

In the more remote parts of Romania, small pockets of communities survive that seem to have more in common with the Middles Ages than with the twenty-first century. There, the traditional way of work and leisure has continued fairly unchanged. For instance, many people still wear traditional costumes as everyday dress and not just for festive occasions. Even in communities more exposed to modern life, traditional clothes are worn as Sunday best for church.

Leisure activities in the villages are usually centered on the family and the village community. Sunday afternoons are devoted to village dances, either in the village square or on specially built platforms. A typical dance is the *hora* (HOR-rah), where participants gather around holding each other's shoulders and dance in a series of easy steps to the accompaniment of music. Food and drink are plentiful, as the women of the village get together to cook for the event. Leisure time is also spent on crafts such as embroidery, pottery, woodcarving, and quilt-making.

Children make the most out of a flooded field near their home in Rast, Romania, in makeshift boats on a sunny day.

During the communist Ceausescu regime, it was official policy to create the New Man—a model citizen emerging from a forced mixing of workers from agricultural and proletarian backgrounds. This new hybrid citizen was to be the building block for Romania's bright new future in the twenty-first century. To create this New Man, Ceausescu used a systematization policy in which whole villages were razed to the ground, and the residents resettled in concrete agro-industrial complexes. Traditional patterns of work and leisure were destroyed and replaced by an imposed regimentation that bore little resemblance to the indigenous culture of the people.

An example of enforced leisure was the Cantarea Romaniei *(can-TAH-rah RO-ma-NEE-ah) ("Singing Romania") displays that took place in huge stadiums or on open hillsides to which hundreds of peasants had been transported. This effort was to make the event appear natural and authentic. The people were dressed in folk costumes and performed song and dance routines that were supposed to represent people relaxing and enjoying themselves. Such shows were recorded and televised across the country on weekends. Therefore, Romanians relaxing at home and watching television had little choice but to watch such this sort of entertainment.*

In rural communities, popular folktales are kept alive and passed on to the younger generation by word of mouth rather than through books. A typical folktale contains a moral or reflects aspects of human nature. Hence the traditional customs or culture and the wisdom of the elders in these close-knit communities are passed on to the young by storytelling.

MEDIA MATTERS

Watching television occupies a large portion of many people's free time. Before 1989 there were two channels, and one of these virtually closed down in 1985 as it was restricted to only two hours of cultural programs a day. The content of the main channel included news programs and patriotic songs, with politically correct dramas and documentaries about increasing productivity in factories.

NADIA COMANECI *(1961–)* *It was a long time ago now, but Nadia Comaneci's Olympic achievement in 1976 is still hailed as one of the greatest moments in Olympic history. Comaneci was a fourteen-year-old Romanian gymnast at the Montreal Summer Games when she astounded the world by becoming the first female gymnast to earn a perfect score of 10 for her routine. The scoreboard could not even display the score because a 10.00 was thought to be impossible, and the board did not have spaces for four digits. By the time the Olympics were over, Comaneci had earned seven perfect scores. She took home three gold medals, one silver, and one bronze. She also set several other records and became world famous.*

This was during the reign of Nicolae Ceausescu, and Romanians were forbidden to leave the country without permission, never mind actually emigrate to another country. The communist regime was careful not to let their golden girl get away, but in 1989, just weeks before the revolution, Comaneci escaped her homeland. She ended up in the United States, where she eventually married Bart Conners, a well-known American gymnast.

ILIE NASTASE *(1946–)* *In the 1970s, Ilie Nastase was one of the top tennis players in the world, and ranked number one from 1973 to 1974. Born in Bucharest, he was nicknamed the Bucharest Buffoon because in addition to being a superb athlete, he also enjoyed entertaining the crowds with his antics—as well as tantrums—on the court. He won seven Grand Slam titles, the most prestigious championship in tennis, and many others. He is one of only five tennis players in the world to win more than one hundred pro titles. He retired in 1985 and in 1991 was inducted into the International Tennis Hall of Fame.*

In addition to his speed and playing style, Nastase was known for his good looks, and is—or at least was—reportedly quite a ladies' man. The athlete married his fourth wife, a Romanian fashion model, in 2013.

GHEORGHE HAGI (1965–) *Nicknamed Regele ("The King"), Commandante ("The Commander"), and the "Maradona of the Carpathians" (after Argentine soccer superstar Diego Maradona), Gheorghe Hagi is considered by many to be the greatest Romanian soccer player of all times. He played professionally during the 1980s and 1990s, spending three seasons with the team Steaua Bucharest before joining the Spanish team Real Madrid. He went on to play for other international teams as well, but is also remembered for leading the Romania team to its best ever international performance, when the team made it to the quarter finals of the 1994 World Cup.*

In 2009, he opened the Gheorghe Hagi Football Academy, a soccer club, to nurture young Romanian talent.

Romania now has cable and satellite TV, delivering a wide variety of channels, both state and private. Antenna 1 is Romania's first commercial network and offers a wide variety of programs. Pro-TV is one of the most popular local channels, while teenagers and hip Romanians catch the latest music videos on Atomic TV. Lack of funding has seen many of Romania's television stations come under Western control. This has led to a flood of Western programming, not all of it good quality, being broadcast in Romania.

Radio has also changed since the introduction of private radio stations. One of the first to be established was Radio Fun, helped by Belgium's private radio station of the same name. Radio Contact, based in Bucharest, broadcasts the news in English and plays Western pop music and some Romanian music. The radio waves are filled with choices; today there are more than one hundred stations.

Before the revolution, newspapers in Romania were characterized by their dullness and predictability. Although there was more than one newspaper, the news was exactly the same except for the sports coverage that had a degree of independent reporting. Censorship meant that a uniform version of home and international news was presented to everyone on radio and television.

In recent years the number of newspapers and magazines available to Romanians has grown tremendously, and there are more than half a dozen independent national papers. Minority-language newspapers are also available in some areas. The Romanian *Magyar Szó* is the main Hungarian-language daily, and the German *Deutsche Zeitung* is published weekly.

In 2014, Reporters Without Borders, an international group which champions freedom of the press, freedom of expression, and journalist safety, ranked Romania number 45 out of 180 on its World Press Freedom Index, a position which it rates as "satisfactory." (For comparison, Finland was rated number 1 and Eritrea was last; the United States came in just under Romania at number 46.) Romania's position fell three points, according to the group, because in 2013, the Romanian parliament recriminalized the acts of insult and libel, which had been decriminalized in 2006. Human rights activists say this means people can be imprisoned for their words, which is not the way democracies are supposed to function.

SPORTS

A very popular game played by young people, mainly in the countryside, is *oina* (OY-nah), a cross between baseball and cricket. The game, which dates back as far as the fourteenth century, is played on a field with a bat and a leather ball. A player on one team throws the ball and a player on the opposing team hits it. Oina is played in schools, as are soccer (called football) and basketball, and a wide variety of other sports.

Though oina is a homegrown game, the undisputed favorite sport in Romania, as it is throughout Europe, is soccer. The Romanian Football Federation (FRF) is the sport's national governing body. Domestic play is organized in a four-tier league system made up of Liga I, Liga II, Liga III, and various county leagues. There are three major cup competitions: the Cupa

Romaniei, which is open to all Romanian professional soccer clubs, the Supercupa Romaniei, which matches the champions of Liga I and the winners of the Cupa Romaniei, and the Cupa Ligii.

Tennis, rugby, handball, and gymnastics are also popular in Romania. Basketball is particularly favored by young people. In addition, Romanians enjoy outdoor activities such as hiking, cycling, exploring caves, and fishing. Along the Black Sea coast, people take part in canoeing and other water sports. The mountains provide skiing, with the most popular of Romania's ski resorts being Sinaia in the Bucegi Mountains and Poiana Brasov in the Carpathians.

An oina player swings for the ball in this traditional Romanian game.

INTERNET LINKS

www.fifa.com/associations/association=rou
The International Football Federation (FIFA) has a page devoted to the Romanian teams.

www.atpworldtour.com/Tennis/Players/Na/I/Ilie-Nastase.aspx
The Pro Tennis World Tour site has a bio of Ilie Nastase.

www.dailymail.co.uk/femail/article-2711049/The-terrifying-day-I-defected-NAdia-Comaneci-tells-harrowing-story.html
This story from 2014 about Nadia Comaneci includes a photo gallery and embedded video of her perfect balance beam performance at the 1976 Olympics.

www.poianabrasov.com
The site of this well-known Romanian mountain resort has information in and real-time weather reports in English.

en.rsf.org/romania.html
The Reporters Without Borders site lists articles relating to Romania.

FESTIVALS

Actors portray Romeo and Juliet at the International Festival of Statues in Bucharest.

BLUES FESTIVALS, MARATHONS, wine expos, international film festivals, mountain bike races, motor sports races, an electronic dance music festival, ballet competitions, tennis tournaments, gay pride parades, Jazz in the Park, International Jazz Day, jazz festivals, jazz, jazz, and more jazz—this is Romania? Of course! Romanians live in the twenty-first century just like everyone else, and they enjoy a wide variety of festivities.

The National Festival of Easter Eggs, the Village's Hardest Working Farmer Celebration, the Cheese Polenta and Blues Festival, the Romanian Peasant Museum's Summer Fair, the Parade of Traditional Costumes, the Shepherd's Measuring of Milk Production, the Festival of Goulash and Plum Brandy, the Cheese and Plum Brandy Festival, the Jellied Meat Festival—oh yes, this is Romania as well.

Romania has a rich store of festivals that includes deeply religious events, such as Easter, and ancient secular ones originating in the country's pagan past. It is mainly in the countryside that traditional festivals and celebrations are observed. In different parts of the country, even within different towns in the same region, the various communities have their unique way of celebrating key moments in a year.

12

Sighisoara (See-ghee-SWAHR-ah), a town in Transylvania, hosts an annual medieval festival each July. The ancient Saxon village, the birthplace of Vlad Dracula (Vlad the Impaler), provides the perfect backdrop. The town is also a UNESCO World Heritage Site.

A Christmas tree lights up the night in Brasov center.

Great Union Day, December 1, celebrates the 1918 union of Romania with Transylvania, one of twelve official public holidays on the Romanian calendar. Unification Day, January 24, marks the day of the political union of Walachia and Moldavia in 1862, the foundation of modern Romania.

CHRISTMAS AND THE NEW YEAR

The first event in Romania's Christmas and New Year celebrations is Saint Nicholas' Day on December 6. Animals are slaughtered in preparation for the family feasts on this day. Young people begin their own preparations by resurrecting costumes or making new ones, and rehearsals begin for the *colinde* (CO-lin-deh), the singing of traditional songs outside people's homes on the night before Christmas to wish good luck for the new year.

In rural parts of Moldavia, a goat procession marks the end of one year and the beginning of another. The goat is depicted by a person suitably costumed to resemble the animal. Part of the facial mask includes a jaw socket that can be moved up and down to the accompaniment of music. The clacking sound that this movement produces represents the death pangs of the dying old year.

Another tradition at the end of the year involves a plow, decorated with green leaves to symbolize fertility and growth, being pulled from house to house and cutting a symbolic furrow in front of the family home to bring the inhabitants good luck and prosperity in the new year. The ritual is done to the accompaniment of music; in Transylvania, a choir accompanies the plowers.

In northern Moldavia, January 1 is celebrated with the help of a special instrument that resembles an open barrel. It is drawn along the ground so as to make a loud sound, the significance of which has been lost over time. Sometimes the dragging of the barrel is accompanied by small troupes of players enacting mimes and dressed like bears and goats.

EASTER

Easter is the most important religious festival in Romania. The starting point is Palm Sunday, celebrating the day Jesus rode into Jerusalem on a donkey. On that day, small branches or pussy willows are distributed in churches and hung at home. The following week, the Week of Sufferings, and Lent, a period of forty days prior to Good

Romanians celebrate Easter in Poienile Izei.

Friday, is an important time of devout prayer and fasting for Christians that simulates the time Jesus was preparing for his own death. While Good Friday remembers the crucifixion of Christ and is a solemn day, Easter Sunday is a joyful occasion, and every Christian church in the country is full of worshipers, particularly during midnight Mass.

Christians usually observe Easter on a Sunday in March or April, depending on the date of the first full moon after the spring equinox. The Eastern Orthodox Church follows the Julian rather than the Gregorian calendar, so Easter in Romania may be celebrated a month apart from Easter in other parts of the world.

SPRING AND SUMMER FESTIVALS

Easter is associated with pagan festivals celebrating the end of winter and the rebirth of a new year. Across Romania there are many celebrations of spring and summer that are not associated with religion, although in the last two decades of the Ceausescu era the intense process of urbanization destroyed many of the rural traditions that marked the end of winter.

One of the festivals that has survived is the Pageant of the Juni, held in the city of Brasov in Transylvania on the first Sunday of May. The word *juni*

Martisor (MAR-tsi-shor) literally means March, and it is the name of an old custom to greet the coming of spring that is still observed in various parts of the country. On March 1, women are presented with simple and inexpensive amulets by men. Although similar to St. Valentine's Day in this respect, the gifts do not necessarily have romantic overtones. The little trinkets, tied with red and white strings—red symbolizes strength, wealth, health, and love; white symbolizes faith, hope, and purity—and worn as a brooch are an expression of friendship and represent good luck for the future.

is from the Latin for young men, and the festival is based around parades of the city's young males dressed in their finest clothes and riding through the city to the accompaniment of a loud brass band. The parades set off from the steps of an old church in the heart of the old historic part of the city. At the end of the procession there is a public feast and more dancing and singing.

The antiquity of the Pageant of the Juni may be seen in the fact that some of the costumes worn have been preserved by families for many generations, and in some cases, go back to the first half of the nineteenth century. One famous shirt worn in the procession has been sewn with over four thousand spangles and weighs nearly 22 pounds (10 kg)!

The summer festival of Sinzienele (sin-ZI-air-nair-leh) is celebrated throughout rural Romania, though each region has its own specific ceremony and rituals. However, they have a common trait: the women gather flowers, leaves, and roots for medicinal use, and also to lure love, wealth, and luck, and to chase away evil spirits. Sinzienele occurs near the summer solstice.

THE SHEEP FEAST

This is a traditional shepherd's folk feast associated with the annual moving of the herds to the high pastures. There they graze under the watchful eyes of shepherds on the lookout for predators such as wolves. The sheep themselves do not belong to the shepherds but to the local inhabitants. A deal is negotiated with the shepherds, who not only guard the animals but also make cheeses for the villagers from the milk. An important part of the festival is the milking of sheep and the measuring of milk in order to ascertain the quantity of cheese to expect from each sheep.

Traditional shepherds milk their sheep in Casolt .They will make cheese from the milk.

The festivities vary according to district, but outdoor dances and shepherd-related activities are common features. For example, in some communities, the event opens with a performance known as the Dance of the Girls. The second stage of the festival is signaled by the oldest shepherd. There follows a lively scene as groups of men go through the motions of milking a flock of sheep and measuring out the milk into wooden pails. The men dress for the festival in waist-length sheepskin jackets that are decorated with embroidery and colored tassels. Body searches are playfully carried out to ensure that no one is secretly trying to obtain a higher rating by diluting their quota of milk with water.

After the event, the community feasts on cheese, local meat dishes—especially mutton—and plum brandy. The feast comes to an end with a display of folk dancing and singing.

MUSIC FESTIVALS

Under communist rule classical music was heavily subsidized by the state, so every large town had its own orchestra and full-time conductor. As in the case of sports, parents were keen to encourage any musical talent that their children might possess because this was one of the few ways a young Romanian could leave the country.

November 30, Saint Andrew's Day, is a national holiday for the country's patron saint, and on that night, folk tradition has it that the souls of the dead come back to roam the earth. On the Night of the Vampires, the undead dance at the crossroads or near abandoned houses. In some villages, people guard their houses with garlic, putting cloves on all the windowsills to keep the vampires away. There may be a party that lasts all night, in which the young people take a pot of garlic outside and dance around it by candlelight to protect themselves and their families against illnesses or spells. During the night, tradition says animals will speak with human voices, but any human caught listening is doomed—so naturally no one ever hears these supernatural conversations. Also

Tourists admire Bran Castle.

on this magical night, young girls may discover the identity of their future husband by peering into a fountain by candlelight and seeing his reflection in the water.

The celebration of Halloween on October 31 is catching on in some places in Romania, most likely due to the allure of the Dracula story. Tourists come to Romania in search of a Dracula experience, and spooky events are planned on Halloween night to satisfy such expectations. For example, Bran Castle in Transylvania hosts a Halloween party for horror and mystery fans, in which "Count Dracula" himself leads a tour through the castle.

Dracula souvenirs are available at the Bran Castle shop.

Romania has two major classical music festivals named in honor of Dinu Lipatti, a pianist of the mid-twentieth century, and George Enescu, the country's most famous composer and conductor. The Dinu Lipatti International Piano Competition is held during the month of May and takes place in a different city each year. The George Enescu International Festival is held in Bucharest every three years.

Folk music festivals are more common and are organized in all parts of the country throughout the year, especially in August to coincide with harvest festivals. One of the biggest festivals, known as the Songs of the Olt, takes place in the town of Calimanesti in Walachia.

In George Enescu Square, a free classical music concert draws a large crowd at the Bucharest Music and Film Festival.

INTERNET LINKS

actmedia.eu/daily/st-andrew-s-day-santandrei-a-popular-and-legal-holiday/43417
"St. Andrew's Day—Santandrei—a popular and legal holiday" explains the folkloric and religious rituals associated with this day in Romania.

romaniatourism.com/festivals-events.html
An up-to-date calendar of festivals and events is listed on this Romania tourism site.

romaniatourism.com/sighisoara.html
An overview of the attractions in Sighisoara (and many other notable Romanian places) can be found here.

FOOD

Chimney cakes, a traditional bread-like treat, are cooked over coals and then often decorated with nuts and sugars.

13

ROMANIAN CUISINE IS ALL ABOUT hearty, meaty peasant dishes, with pork being the most popular meat. Bacon, sausages, meatballs and other ground meat dishes, ham hocks, pork roasts, stews, pork rinds, and pig trotters all have a welcome spot on the typical Romanian table. Beef, poultry, and mutton (lamb) are also loved. These dishes reflect the history and heritage of its people, with Roman, Greek, Turkish, and German influences. Cabbage, beets, sour cream, sheep's cheese, soured and pickled foods, and cornmeal polenta are regulars, as they are in other Eastern European cuisines.

Romania's national dish, if it can be said to have one, would probably be stuffed cabbage rolls served with polenta and sour cream, perhaps with a little pickled pepper on the side. And for dessert? That could depend on the region—in the west, it might be apple strudel; in other areas, crepes filled with chocolate or fresh fruit might be the sweet of choice.

In Transylvania, Hungarian influences show up in the cuisine. People here like their food a bit spicier and paprika, a favorite Hungarian spice, is often added to traditional Romanian recipes.

FOLK DISHES

Mamaliga (mah-me-LI-ga), or polenta, is the staple food of Romanians in all parts of the country, and in the countryside it is eaten cold for breakfast. It is a thick cornmeal mush that is served in a variety of ways. As a side dish to the main meal, it's kind of like mashed potatoes, a soft, bland comfort food that goes with meat and vegetable dishes. Mamaliga is traditionally prepared with a *facalet* (fah-KEH-letz), a wooden stick somewhat like a rolling pin with the top sometimes carved with an individual design and the owner's name. Another important staple food in Romania is bread.

The best dishes in Romania come from the countryside. *Tocana* (to-KANA), which means stew, is like a borsch soup and is a very popular meal in rural areas. The usual meat used is chicken or mutton, and tocana is flavored with onions and garlic. Vegetables in the stew include potatoes, carrots, peppers, and beans. It is still the practice just before winter in rural areas to bury vegetables in a deep hole in the ground that is covered with leaves and straw. When snow falls, the vegetables are preserved until early spring.

A tocana, a traditional meat and vegetable stew, cooks over a fire.

THE BAD OLD DAYS

During the communist era, Romanian meals were very different. Fresh vegetables were mostly unobtainable, and items like bread and cheese were scarce. A standard meal for many families was a thin broth made from rice and chicken or pig's bones.

Shopping for food was a demoralizing experience. Not only were standard items frequently rationed, but the shortage of basic foodstuffs encouraged and maintained a widespread black market (secret, illegal sales). It was common practice for staff in food shops to keep some food off the shelves and sell them later when supplies were no longer available. Shopkeepers knew they could fetch a higher price by selling the foodstuffs in the black market.

Menus in restaurants might list half a dozen different meals, but in reality only one might be available because the ingredients were simply not obtainable. The only people who could have full meals regularly were groups of tourists on package tours who stayed at

During the food shortage, a butcher comes out of his shop to inform the long line that he is out of meat.

special tourist hotels. The reality of the food situation was kept hidden from them. At the time, Romania was exporting large quantities of food in an attempt to pay off the country's accumulated foreign debts. Meat was often available only through the black market, and the only Romanians who could eat well were high-ranking members of the government.

Two pieces of mititei are served with mustard.

Pork mixed with beef, or sometimes lamb, is also used to make grilled meatballs known as *mititei* (me-tee-TAY), a word that comes from the word for small. They resemble small hamburgers or are cylindrical in shape and have a spicier taste. By tradition they are broiled outdoors over charcoal and served hot with red or green peppers and sour pickles flavored with dill. Mititei is often eaten as a snack or as an appetizer with mustard and is consumed with a glass of wine or beer. Mititei is sold by street vendors in the cities.

Ciorba (CHOR-ba) is a sour soup, with the traditional sour base made from the fermented juice of wheat bran. It takes time to prepare the soup, and nowadays Romanians tend to use unripened green grapes, green sorrel leaves, or lemon juice, instead of fermenting wheat bran. *Ciorba de burta* ("tripe soup"), served with garlic or hot chili pepper and vinegar, is a particular favorite.

Sarmale (sar-MALL-eh), or stuffed cabbage rolls, a dish of Armenian and Greek origin, is very popular throughout the country. It consists of cabbage or grape leaves stuffed with rice, meat, and herbs. The filling can be cooked in tomato or lemon sauce, and sarmale is sometimes served with cream.

The most common desserts in Romania are pancakes and *placinte* (pla-CHIN-te), which are like crepe suzettes or turnovers in North America. The Turkish influence on Romanian food is apparent in the fondness for baklava, a pastry with crushed pistachios or almonds glazed with thick honey syrup.

Torte (TOHRT), a variety of rich cake, is becoming more common since the ingredients are more easily available. It used to be made by young village girls who took turns meeting at one of their kitchens on a Sunday afternoon to make the dessert together.

DRINK

Tuica (TSUI-kuh), a brandy usually made from plums, is the national alcoholic drink. A glass is customarily drunk neat, without adding water or fruit juice, before meals and at festivities. At weddings, tuica is often the main drink.

Sometimes it is made from pears and other fruits. In Transylvania, *palinca* (pal-INK-ka) is the Hungarian equivalent of tuica. It is distilled twice and is far more potent.

Romania has a long tradition in wine-growing. In the nineteenth century, Polish princes used to buy Romanian wines and escort the wine back to Poland with drawn swords as though they were transporting gold. Wines from the Murfatlar region in southeastern Romania have won many European wine awards. Generally, a bottle of wine is not very expensive in Romania.

Coffee is far more popular than tea. The reason for the popularity of coffee may be the legacy of Turkey's historical influence over the country. Coffee is usually taken black and very sweet, as is the custom in Turkey.

A sampling of palinca at the Cheese and Tuica Festival.

INTERNET LINKS

www.lonelyplanet.com/romania/travel-tips-and-articles/a-guide-to-romanian-cuisine
This Lonely Planet article is a good overview of Romanian cuisine.

www.romanianmonasteries.org/romania/romanian-food
This page features a long list of Romanian foods with some photos and recipes.

SARMALE (STUFFED CABBAGE ROLLS)

Romanians typically use whole cabbages that have been prepared in advance like sauerkraut, but you can use fresh cabbage, though it will need blanching. For authentic taste, add prepared sauerkraut to the recipe.

1 and a half pounds ground meat
  (combination beef and pork)
3 Tbsp rice, uncooked
1 onion, finely chopped
2 Tbsp chopped fresh dill or parsley
1 or 2 slices of crustless white bread, soaked in water and squeezed out and mashed
1 large or 2 small fresh cabbages (or 1 fresh cabbage and 1 quart of sauerkraut)
2 Tbsp olive oil
salt, pepper
15-ounce can tomato sauce, diluted with one can of water
6—8 strips of bacon, lightly sautéed
sour cream

Remove tough outer leaves from fresh cabbage. Blanch cabbage to soften leaves: Bring a large pot of water to a boil. Stick a sharp two-pronged fork into the cabbage core and submerge the cabbage in the boiling water. As the outer leaves soften, after a half minute or so, remove leaves with a pair of tongs to a bowl of cold water. Continue until you have removed as many leaves as you can.

Mix the ground meat with chopped onion, the soaked and mashed bread, the rice, herbs, salt and pepper. Loosen mixture with a couple of tablespoons of water.

Drain the cabbage leaves. Cut out center rib. Fill each leaf with a spoonful of the ground meat mixture and roll, tucking in the ends of the cabbage leaf. If the leaves are very big, cut them in half. The bundles should look like eggrolls.

(continued)

Oil a large baking pan. Finely chop the remaining cabbage, mix with sauerkraut, and spread a layer on the bottom of the pan. Top with half the bacon, broken into pieces. Add one half of tomato sauce mixture. Arrange cabbage rolls, lined up in neat rows (in layers if necessary). Cover with remaining bacon and tomato sauce. If rolls are not completely submerged, add boiling water to cover.

Cover pan tightly with lid or foil and cook in oven for about 1 and a half to 2 hours.

Serve with mamaliga (polenta) and sour cream.

MAMALIGA (ROMANIAN-STYLE POLENTA)

1 qt water
2 tsp salt
2 Tbsp butter
1 cup yellow corn meal

Boil water, butter, and salt in a pot. When water is boiling, gradually add corn meal while stirring the mixture with a whisk. Lower heat and simmer until mixture thickens; at least ten or fifteen minutes, or more depending on your cornmeal. Use caution since the mixture bubbles up and splatters as it simmers. If you wish, stir in more butter, a handful of feta cheese, a dollop of sour cream, or a sprinkle of herbs. Remove from the heat and serve hot with your favorite dish.

MAP OF ROMANIA

ECONOMIC ROMANIA

Agriculture

 Grain

 Livestock

 Wine

Services

 Airport

 Port

 Tourism

Manufacturing

 Food Products

 Paper Products

 Ship Building

 Textiles

 Wood Products

Natural Resources

 Coal

 Fish

 Oil

 Salt

 Timber

ABOUT THE ECONOMY

OVERVIEW

Economic gains since 1989 have only recently started to spur creation of a middle class and to address Romania's widespread poverty. Corruption and red tape continue to permeate the business environment. After the 2008 global financial crisis, Romania received a $26 billion emergency assistance loan from the IMF, EU, and World Bank. Economic growth picked up in 2013, and the country was able to pay off much of its loan.

GROSS DOMESTIC PRODUCT (GDP)

$288.5 billion (2013)

GDP SECTORS

Services 59.4 percent; industry 34.2 percent; agriculture 6.4 percent (2013)

LAND AREA

92,043 square miles (238,391 sq km)

WORKFORCE

9.45 million (2013)

WORKFORCE BY OCCUPATION

Agriculture 29 percent; industry 28.6 percent; services 42.4 percent (2012)

CURRENCY

Romanian leu (RON) (plural: lei)
Notes: 1, 5, 10, 50, 100, 200, 500 lei

Coins: 1, 5, 10, 50 bani
USD 1 = RON 3.60 (December 2014)

INFLATION RATE

1.3 percent (December 2014)

UNEMPLOYMENT RATE

7.1 percent (2014)

NATURAL RESOURCES

Gold, silver, salt, natural gas, oil, coal, lignite, iron, manganese, feldspar, pyrite, marble, graphite, bauxite, mica, timber

AGRICULTURAL PRODUCTS

Wheat, corn, barley, sugar beets, sunflower seed, potatoes, grapes; eggs, sheep

INDUSTRIAL PRODUCTS

Electric machinery and equipment, textiles and footwear, light machinery, auto assembly, mining, timber, construction materials, metallurgy, chemicals, food processing, petroleum refining

MAJOR TRADE PARTNERS

Germany, Italy, Hungary, France, Turkey, Russia (2012)

MAJOR EXPORTS

Textiles, footwear, chemicals, metals and metal products, machinery and equipment, minerals, fuels

MAJOR IMPORTS

Machinery and equipment, chemicals, fuels and minerals, metals, textile and products, agricultural products

CULTURAL ROMANIA

Sighet Prison
During communist times, the Sighet Prison in Sighetu Maramatiei was known as the Prison of the Ministers for its political inmates. Now empty of its prisoners, it reopened in 1997 as the Memorial Museum of the Victims of Communism and Anti-Communist Resistance.

Sucevita Monastery
Built by the princes Simion and Ieremia Movila between 1582 and 1584, the massive, fortified Sucevita Monastery in Moldavia is famous for the vivid frescoes that cover much of its interior. The tombs of the monastery's founders lie within. During communist rule, only nuns older than fifty were allowed to stay at the monastery.

Baile Herculane
Legend has it that Hercules bathed in the springs here to heal the wounds caused by the Hydra. The first baths were built by Roman legions after their conquest of the Dacians and in the nineteenth century, Baile Herculane in Caras Severin became a fashionable resort.

Danube Delta
The Danube Delta has the largest reed beds in the world and a large population of wildlife. Hundreds of migratory and native birds nest on the delta, including endangered species such as the great white egret and the white-tailed eagle, making the delta an excellent place for bird watching.

Apuseni Mountains
The Apuseni Mountains in the Western Carpathians are renowned for their extensive cave systems lined with large limestone formations. The Cetatile Ponorului is one of the most impressive cave systems. Carved by a river, it cuts through an entire mountain, creating a natural bridge.

Sighisoara
Settled by the Saxons in the twelfth century, Sighisoara in Transylvania is considered the most complete site of medieval architecture in Romania. Much of the old town or citadel is in good condition and nine of the original fourteen towers remain. Vlad III of Dracula legend was born in Sighisoara around 1431.

Retezat National Park
Located in the Hunedoara in the southwestern Transylvania Carpathians, the country's first national park and a UNESCO Biosphere Reserve is home to around three hundred plant species and numerous animals, such as the brown bear, wolf, fox, and deer.

Palace of Parliament
Located in Bucharest, the Palace of Parliament is the second-largest building in the world in surface area and is a massive example of Ceausescu's megalomania in the 1980s. It is 885 feet by 787 feet (270 m x 240 m) and 282 feet (86 m) high, with a surface area of 3.6 million square feet (330,000 sq m).

Tropaeum Traiani
Near the town of Adamclisi is a reconstruction of the Tropaeum Traiani. The original monument was built in 106–109 BCE to commemorate Trajan's conquest of the Dacians. Scenes from the battle are depicted at the base.

ABOUT THE CULTURE

COUNTRY NAME
Romania

CAPITAL
Bucharest

OTHER MAJOR CITIES
Brasov, Cluj-Napoca, Constanta, Iasi, Timisoara

GOVERNMENT
Republic

POPULATION
21,729,871 (2014)

NATIONAL FLAG
Three vertical bands of blue, yellow, and red

NATIONAL ANTHEM
"Awaken Thee, Romanian!"
("Desteapta-te, Romane!"). Poem written by Andrei Muresianu in 1848; music by Anton Pann

ETHNIC GROUPS
Romanian 83.4 percent, Hungarian 6.1 percent, Roma 3.1 percent, Ukrainian 0.3 percent, German 0.2 percent, other 0.7 percent, unspecified 6.1 percent (2011)

RELIGIONS
Eastern Orthodox 81.9 percent, Protestant 6.4 percent, Roman Catholic 4.3 percent, other (includes Muslim) 0.9 percent, none or atheist 0.2 percent, unspecified 6.3 percent (2011)

OFFICIAL LANGUAGE
Romanian

LITERACY RATE
97.7 percent (2011)

NATIONAL HOLIDAYS
New Year (January 1 and 2), Easter Monday (March/April), Unification Day (December 1), Christmas (December 25 and 26).

LEADERS IN POLITICS
Victor Ponta, prime minister, 2012—
Klaus Iohannis, president, 2014—

TIMELINE

IN ROMANIA	IN THE WORLD
700 BCE The Dacian civilization develops.	**753 BCE** Rome is founded.
106 CE The Romans conquer Dacia.	**116–17 BCE** The Roman Empire reaches its greatest extent, under Emperor Trajan (98–17).
600–900 CE The Slavs and Magyars move into Dacia.	**600 CE** Height of Mayan civilization
1003 Transylvania becomes a part of the Hungarian Kingdom.	**1000** The Chinese perfect gunpowder and begin to use it in warfare.
1330 The state of Walachia is formed.	
1359 Moldavia achieves independence.	
1434 Ottoman Empire advances into Dacia.	
	1530 Beginning of transatlantic slave trade organized by the Portuguese in Africa
1600 Michael the Brave briefly unites Walachia, Moldavia, and Transylvania. The next year Romania is formally recognized as a state.	**1558–1603** Reign of Elizabeth I of England **1620** Pilgrims sail the *Mayflower* to America.
1699 Transylvania comes under the Habsburg kingdom.	
1711 Greek Phanariot rule begins.	**1776** US Declaration of Independence
	1789–99 The French Revolution
1859 Alexandru Cuzu is elected ruler of both Moldavia and Walachia.	**1861** The US Civil War begins.
1866 First Romanian constitution is created.	**1869** The Suez Canal is opened.
1877 Romania formally becomes independent.	
1881 Romania is recognized as a kingdom.	

IN ROMANIA	IN THE WORLD
	1914
1920	World War I begins.
Transylvania is returned to Romania.	**1939**
1940	World War II begins.
Northern Transylvania is ceded to Hungary and other territories to the Soviet Union.	
1945	**1945**
Soviet-backed government is installed.	WWII ends.
1947	**1949**
Romania regains Tranyslvania.	The North Atlantic Treaty Organization (NATO)
Romanian People's Republic is established.	is formed.
1955	
Romania joins the Warsaw Pact.	
	1966–1969
	The Chinese Cultural Revolution
1985–86	**1986**
Nicolae Ceausescu implements austerity program.	Nuclear power disaster at Chernobyl in Ukraine
1989	
Ceausescu is deposed and executed.	
1990	
First elections are held.	**1991**
Ion Iliescu becomes president.	Breakup of the Soviet Union
2000	
Ion Iliescu is reelected as president.	**2001**
	Terrorists crash planes in New York, Washington, DC, and Pennsylvania.
	2003
2004	War in Iraq
Romania joins NATO.	
2007	
Romania and Bulgaria join European Union.	**2008**
2010	United States elects first African American
EU demands Romania take urgent action to tackle crime and corruption.	president, Barak Obama.
2014	
Klaus Iohannis wins presidential election.	**2015**
	In Paris, 3.7 million people march to defy terrorism after an extremist attack.

GLOSSARY

buchium (BU-chium)
Alpenhorn used by shepherds to communicate, now considered a musical instrument.

ciorba (CHOR-ba)
A sour soup made with a broth of fermented wheat bran, lemon juice, or other sour ingredient.

cirque (chirk)
Steep, hollow excavations on mountainsides made by glacial erosion.

colinde (CO-lin-deh)
Traditional songs expressing good luck for the new year that are sung outside homes on Christmas Eve.

collectivization
The ownership and control of the means of production and distribution is given to the people involved instead of a few individuals.

communism
A political, economic, and social system in which all property and resources are collectively owned by the state, and wealth is distributed—theoretically—equally or according to need.

Dacians
Earliest recorded inhabitants, colonized by the Romans between the first and fourth centuries.

Eastern Orthodox Church
A group of churches that recognizes the jurisdiction of the Patriarch of Constantinople; believers of the Eastern Orthodox Church follow the teachings of the church before the schism in the eleventh century.

iconostasis
A decorated screen in Eastern Orthodox churches that separates the sanctuary from the nave.

Magyars
Ethnic Hungarians who originated in Central Asia.

mamaliga (mah-me-LI-ga)
Staple food made from cornmeal.

Phanariots
Greek nobles sent by the Turks to rule Romania in the eighteenth century.

sarmale (sar-MALL-eh)
Stuffed cabbage rolls, the unofficial national dish of Romania.

Tatars
People belonging to the various Mongolian and Turkic tribes, who under Genghis Khan (1162—1227) and his successors ruled parts of central and western Asia and Eastern Europe until the eighteenth century.

tuica (TSUI-kuh)
A type of brandy usually made from plums.

voivodates
Areas under the control of a military leader known as a voivode.

FOR FURTHER INFORMATION

BOOKS

Hitchens, Keith. *A Concise History of Romania.* Cambridge Classic Histories. Cambridge, England: Cambridge University Press, 2014

Imbarus, Aura. *Out of the Transylvania Night.* San Diego: Bettie Youngs Books, 2010

Klepper, Nicolae, *Taste of Romania.* New York: Hippocrene Books, 2011

Molnar, Haya Leah. *Under a Red Sky: Memoir of a Childhood in Communist Romania.* New York: Farrar Straus Giroux, 2010

Stowe, Debbie. *Romania.* Culture Smart! London: Bravo Ltd., 2008

VIDEOS

Across the Forest: Tales from Transylvania. Justin Blair and Matthew Vincent, 2009.

Count Dracula (BBC Mini-Series), BBC Home Entertainment, 2007.

Lost and Found: The Story of Romania's Forgotten Children, Documentary Educational Resources, 1992.

Passport to Adventure: Bucharest & the Transylvanian Countryside Romania, Cinergy Productions, 2009.

WEBSITES

BBC News Europe. "Romania Profile." www.bbc.com/news/world-europe-17776265

CIA World Factbook, Romania. www.cia.gov/library/publications/the-world-factbook/geos/ro.html

Embassy of Romania to the United States of America. washington.mae.ro/en

Lonely Planet, Romania. www.lonelyplanet.com/romania

Romania.org. www.romania.org

Romania Tourism. romaniatourism.com

The New York Times. "Romania."
topics.nytimes.com/top/news/international/countriesandterritories/romania/index.html

UNESCO World Heritage Sites, Romania. whc.unesco.org/en/statesparties/ro

BIBLIOGRAPHY

Bauer, Markus. "Coming to Terms with the Past: Romania." *History Today*, February 2007. www.historytoday.com/markus-bauer/coming-terms-past-romania

Chelminski, Rudy. "The Curse of Count Dracula." *Smithsonian Magazine*, April 2003. www.smithsonianmag.com/travel/the-curse-of-count-dracula-79837910/?no-ist

European Commission ERAWATCH, "Romania: Higher Education Institutions" erawatch.jrc.ec.europa.eu/erawatch/opencms/information/country_pages/ro/country?section=ResearchPerformers&subsection=HigherEducationInstitutions

Ghosh, Palash. "Medical Leave: Romanian Doctors Fleeing Poor Pay, Corruption For Western Europe," *International Business Times*, February 21, 2014. www.ibtimes.com/medical-leave-romanian-doctors-fleeing-poor-pay-corruption-western-europe-1557178

Higgins, Andrew, "In Trial, Romania Warily Revisits a Brutal Past," *The New York Times*, Sept. 29, 2013. www.nytimes.com/2013/09/30/world/europe/in-trial-romania-warily-revisits-a-brutal-past.html?pagewanted=all

Higgins, Andrew. "Russian Money Suspected Behind Fracking Protests," *The New York Times*, Nov. 30, 2014. www.nytimes.com/2014/12/01/world/russian-money-suspected-behind-fracking-protests.html

Holeywell, Ryan. "Romania pitches itself as next big thing in energy," *Houston Chronicle*, Sept. 26, 2014. www.houstonchronicle.com/business/article/Romania-pitches-itself-as-next-big-thing-in-energy-5784113.php#/0

Legatum Prosperity Index. www.prosperity.com

Steavenson, Wendell. "Ceausescu's Children," *The Guardian*, Dec. 10, 2014. www.theguardian.com/news/2014/dec/10/-sp-ceausescus-children

United States Embassy in Bucharest. romania.usembassy.gov

US Energy Information Administration, "Romania Overview," August 2014. www.eia.gov/countries/country-data.cfm?fips=ro

World Bank Group, Romania Partnership, "Country Program Snapshot," October 2014, www.worldbank.org/content/dam/Worldbank/document/eca/Romania-Snapshot.pdf

INDEX

INDEX